COMMON
SENSE MINISTRY
MULTIPLIED

Also by James A. Cress

Common Sense Ministry

More Common Sense Ministry

You Can Keep Them If You Care

JAMES A. CRESS

COMMON
SENSE MINISTRY
MULTIPLIED

Pacific Press® Publishing Association
Nampa, Idaho
Oshawa, Ontario, Canada
www.pacificpress.com

Cover design by Gerald Lee Monks
Cover design resources from the author's family.
Inside design by Aaron Troia

You can obtain additional copies of this book by calling toll-free 1-800-765-6955 or by visiting http://www.adventistbookcenter.com.

Library of Congress Cataloging-in-Publication Data:

Cress, James A.
  Common sense ministry multiplied / James A. Cress.
    p. cm.
  Articles originally appeared as author's columns in *Ministry* magazine.
  ISBN 13: 978-0-8163-2411-8 (pbk.)
  ISBN 10: 0-8163-2411-5 (pbk.)
  1. Pastoral theology. 2. Church work. I. Ministry (Washington, D.C.)
II. Title.
  BV4011.3.C74 2010
  253—dc22
                                                          2010010196

10 11 12 13 14 • 5 4 3 2 1

Dedication

From Jim, who loved Jesus dearly,
served Him tirelessly through word and deed,
and ministered to His ministers by empowering them and their spouses
in every possible way,
comes this work—a selection
from his Pastor's Pastor column in *Ministry,*
sharing the joys and challenges of ministry
during seventeen years of leadership to the world church.
This book is a labor of faith, hope, and love.
It is dedicated to all those who continue spreading the gospel of Jesus
until we are all united with Him.

In that everlasting hope,
Sharon

For I am persuaded, that neither death,

nor life, nor angels, nor principalities, nor powers,

nor things present, nor things to come,

nor height, nor depth, nor any other creature,

shall be able to separate us from the love of God,

which is in Christ Jesus our Lord.

—Romans 8:38, 39, KJV

Table of Contents

SECTION IV: REACHING IN

SECTION V: REACHING TOGETHER

Foreword

He came young, focused, and dynamic.

When Jim Cress was elected by the 1992 Annual Council of the world church as the eighth and youngest-ever ministerial association secretary of the General Conference, he assumed the office with the dreams of the youth and the vision of the experienced. The dream and the vision defined his ministry as he circled the world to transform the meaning and methods of the pastors, to equip those pastors and the supporting spouses with a Spirit-filled charge and the needed tools of the ministry, and to work methodically to help the church leadership to recognize and honor the pivotal role of the pastor in an ever-changing world with a never-changing message.

"Pastoring is a privilege of grace," Jim wrote in a momentous definition of ministry as he embraced and practiced it. Those words in his first signature column, "Pastor's Pastor," in *Ministry* magazine, drove him literally to the ends of the earth, from suitcase to suitcase: leading an evangelistic campaign in Ghana, training a pastoral group with their spouses in Manila, equipping the church in India with funds for volunteer pastoral couples to minister to hundreds of new churches mushrooming all over that challenging country. The global congregation that stretched from Peru to Japan, Papua New Guinea to Russia, became his pastoral burden, moving him to work tirelessly to meet every possible challenge and need. *Call him a pastor with a youthful vision.*

Jim's unceasing focus was twofold—professional and pastoral. As a professional, he saw ministers around the world engaged in evangelism and pastoral care without adequate equipment. From day one of his assumption of the office, he worked without ceasing to meet this desperate need. He raised funds, motivated publishers, and challenged church leaders and administrative committees to provide the tools so that pastors could finish their job. Soon, *Ministry* magazine became available to pastors everywhere, including non-Adventist clergy, *Seventh-day Adventists Believe . . .* was sent to most clergy homes, and an essential ministerial library became affordable— in most cases, for a dollar a book. But perhaps the most prized, cherished love-gift that Jim Cress gave to his fellow pastors, particularly in disadvantaged countries, was his dream project, which was fulfilled within his first two years in office. He saw to it that pastors could purchase the first seven volumes of the *Seventh-day Adventist Bible Commentary* at the unbelievable cost of fifty dollars. Pastors at once had the resources that enabled them to become serious Bible students who proclaimed a serious Bible message every Sabbath.

The pastoral dimension of Jim's life extended to providing a wholistic cast to the ministerial calling. Equipped with a bachelor's degree in theology (Southern Adventist University), a Master of Divinity (Andrews University), a DMin (Fuller Theological Seminary), and eighteen years of service as a pastor and ministerial leader, Jim understood the toil, the sweat, and the reward of the pastoral calling. The road he walked was not paved and smooth, nor the journey he undertook straightforward and comfortable. But early in his work he realized that he was never alone. He always spoke of a Shepherd under whom he was only an under-shepherd. Such a conviction was well expressed in his first *Ministry* column: "Jesus could have done the work of ministry much more effectively than the eleven apostles and few dozen disciples. . . . [But] He risked the future . . . on just those few."

Jim knew he was one of those few, and as a pastor "on loan to the General Conference," he was determined to do his very best for the more than ten thousand pastors around the world. And not for the pastors only. Jim believed and practiced team ministry. From the time he and Sharon were married, in 1970, the two worked as a pastoral team, and the concept has now spread to the world church. Sharon and Jim equipped pastoral couples everywhere to carry on Christ's unfinished business. *Call him a pastor with a focus.*

Jim Cress was a multitasker; he had the gift of profound energy and dynamism. On a single day he could be planning for a large ministerial convention on the other side of the globe, make a conference call with members of the platform committee of the General Conference session, send an e-mail expressing his personal concern to a church member who had lost a loved one, send a card of congratulations to a young couple getting married, mail a birthday card to his high school friend, work on a manuscript, and complete a dozen other tasks—all done with a sense of doing what his Master had invited him to do years ago. *Call him a pastor with a dynamic commitment.*

Young he came to his final place of ministry, and young he was called to rest. Jim Cress died on November 26, 2009, at the age of sixty. But the life of a person is measured not by how long but by how well he lived. By that criterion, Jim lived a full, Spirit-filled, blessed life for the glory of his Lord and for the good of His global family. That we may mark Jim's contribution to ministry, his beloved wife, Sharon, has put together a selection of some of the best of his writings. She has organized and edited this volume with the prayer that it will always remind us that we are pastors on loan to do the Lord's bidding.

John M. Fowler
Associate Editor, *Ministry*
1990–1995

SECTION I:
REACHING UP

Breakaway Pastors

I am not referring to dissident, offshoot pastors who have departed the faith to establish their own independent ministries.

Instead, I'm writing to continuously overworked, overstretched, overextended ministers whose typical response to successful pastoral ministry means doing more of the same with even greater diligence.

One of the greatest reasons for serious reflection about which activities bring success for pastoral ministry may be our inability to distinguish what *busy works* are less effective than others and discard them. If we fail to comprehend which functions do not make us successful, our only recourse for maintaining excellence is doing more of everything until we collapse under the weight of attempting too much.

Let's face it: You probably need a serious breakaway. Of course, a few slackers exist in every profession, including ministry, whose self-starter disengaged years ago and who simply go through the motions of ministry—awaiting the glorious arrival of retirement. These few pastors have much greater potential for rusting out than for burning out. They don't need a vacation; rather, they need a jumpstart to re-envision their potential and to begin functioning at full speed.

On the other hand, the majority of pastors work hard—typically too hard. They need a breakaway. They need a vacation. They do not need one more thing to do. They need the rest, recuperation, restoration, relaxation, renewal, and revival that come only from a sabbatical. In fact, if more Sabbath-teaching pastors were really Sabbath-keeping believers, there would be much less burnout. We even cite Jesus' mention of priests laboring in the temple without breaking the Sabbath commandment—in an effort to excuse our pastoral behavior of working harder on the Lord's Day than any other day of the week.

In that same context, however, we forget Jesus' example of regularly taking meaningful breakaways from His own ministry. And remember, Jesus took these breakaways in full advance knowledge from Daniel 9 that His public ministry would last only three and a half years. Busy as He was, Jesus regularly experienced specific breakaway opportunities.

Spiritual retreats. Although He was so exhausted from meeting the needs of the throngs that He even fell asleep in the bottom of a boat in stormy seas, Jesus also knew the necessity of engaging with heaven in spiritual retreats. Whether late at night or in all-night communion with God or arising a long while before dawn to pray, Jesus consistently experienced spiritual retreats for strength and guidance from His heavenly Father whose will He had come to earth to accomplish.

Social retreats. Jesus also enjoyed relaxing times with friends and family. Often He was present at celebrations, banquets, parties, and wedding feasts. In fact, He so often mixed with sinners that some accused Him of gluttony. He so often partied with sinners that some assumed He was a winebibber. Despite Jesus' unsullied character, He repeatedly sought opportunities to mingle with individuals who quickly realized that His interested focus on their individual needs was as One who desired their good.

Recreational retreats. Sometimes the Savior took a day off just to have fun. He would go fishing with the disciples, enjoy a cookout on the beach, or relax in the fellowship of a hearty meal at the home of Lazarus, Martha, and Mary. If Jesus was around, you knew you would enjoy a good time.

So, follow Jesus' example. Become a breakaway pastor. Experience the blessings of spiritual, social, and recreational retreats. If a weekly day off isn't your thing, then strive to schedule recurring weeklong breaks. In my own ministry, I need a couple weeks' breakaway just to become creative again. After several months of extended work, I find that the first few days of a two-week break bring restorative sleep and virtual mental inactivity as I unwind. Slowly, but surely, as my body rests and my mind clears, the creative process reawakens and I can begin to think in new ways, design fresh projects, and plan bright sermons, articles, or lectures. Creative ideas, which I could never have forced into an overextended schedule or into an overcrowded mind, spring up with surprising freshness once I am rested.

Returned missionary Denele Ivins[1] describes some specific tips for planning such a personal breakaway:

Admit your need for rest. There is no shame in being tired because you are serving others. You are only human.

Put it on the calendar. Once you determine your need for rest, schedule a date on the calendar before it fills up. Stick to it!

Get the support of your family, friends, and members. Share why you need a retreat and ask your friends to pray for you through the process. Recognize that your spouse may carry an extra load while you retreat, so be prepared to reciprocate during your spouse's renewal opportunity.

Resist taking someone along. A personal retreat sounds like such a good idea that others who hear your plan will want to join you. Keep it solo for maximum renewal effectiveness while encouraging others to schedule their own.

Don't feel guilty. While it is true that you are leaving behind needs and tasks, the unselfish thing to do is to make being renewed a priority. You will return strengthened for the tasks at hand.

---

1. Denele Ivins, "Rest for the Weary," *Just Between Us,* Spring 2007, 10.

Customize your retreat. Think through what *restful* means for you. Rustic or luxurious? Active or quiet? Mountains, ocean, or desert? Near or far? Include the nature element. The heavens do declare His glory, and the great outdoors provides the perfect setting in which to be renewed.

Take advantage of resources. Check with your colleagues for retreat venues in your area designed especially for ministry workers. These are usually lower-cost and sometimes offer counseling and other resources. Think creatively. Consider off-season church camps, a friend's cabin, or a place you'd like to visit.

Address the whole person. Include elements of rest and renewal for your body, mind, and soul. Visit a museum, attend a ball game, read a book, take a walk, or ride a riverboat. Just do it!

Take a well-stocked tool chest. Go prepared with your Bible, devotional book, hymnal, and journal. Pack lighter reading and favorite snacks. Retreat is not the time to fast—or even diet.

Have great expectations. Expect God to meet you in a special way. He specializes in giving rest to the weary and just asks us to come!

Fasting

Here we go again, I thought as Pastor Reuben Roundtree Jr. announced that his congregation, for whom I was conducting a short evangelistic series, would experience a week of fasting.

I had not been mistaken for a starving war orphan since I was eight years old. Then, I was so skinny that my mom had to "take up my trousers until the pockets met in the back." Of course, I *needed* to fast, but I dreaded enduring (attempting and failing) days without eating during a heavy schedule of preaching, counseling, visiting, and other appointments.

Imagine my delight when Pastor Roundtree explained that merely to cease eating was far too easy and called instead for various spiritually dynamic fasts in areas where we needed to experience practical changes—food (perhaps), but also shopping, television, Internet surfing, mindless reading, credit cards, workaholism, spectator sports, gossip, and argumentative combat.

Imagine my dismay when just as I responded, "Amen! All right!" the pastor added one other fast—"news media overload." Now that was far too convicting for a news junkie who subscribes to two newspapers plus four major newsweeklies and constantly listens for fresh reports on Cable News Network (CNN). I even have a *Breaking News Alert feature* to interrupt my e-mail.

As the pastor defined fasting in real life practicalities, to have ceased eating would have been far easier than the discipline he advocated. Since then I have contemplated fasting as a spiritual discipline wider than skipping a few meals from time to time.

I have been especially blessed by a new book, *Fasting: Spiritual Freedom Beyond Our Appetites,* by Lynne Babb, which I found time to read only because of a ten-hour flight without any fresh-breaking news. As I write, I'm attempting an entire week's fast from television and news reports assisted by time zone differences from NBC, ABC, or Katie Couric. Here's what I'm discovering.

Satiated life is still "right there." In less than a day, I gravitated to a televised news feature like an addict seeking a fresh fix and found myself eagerly catching up on politics from back home, the latest tragic war report, and the imminent collapse of some business. I even found myself—and I can piously report that I follow no sports—eagerly listening to golf and cricket scores.

Fasting must not derive from an effort to earn meritorious favor. Babb says, "When we fast, we're not trying to impress God. This is not a performance with the goal of manipulating God. God is not a genie in a lamp that we can rub and ask for things. Fasting helps us get in a place where we can hear God" (p. 127).

What am I making room for? At its core, fasting is not a discipline of withholding. It is a discipline of making space for God. Fasting is far more complex and far more significant than merely abstaining from food on a recurring basis. For example, consider spiritual joy. Jesus says, "You're blessed when you've worked up a good appetite for God" (Matthew 5:6, *The Message*).

Scripture does not command fasting. Nowhere does the Bible say, "You must fast." Jesus assumes that His followers will sometimes fast when He gives instructions about how to—or how not to—fast.

Fasting ought to be secret. The Bible talks about groups—even nations—fasting. But Jesus says, "When you fast, do it in secret and do not appear to be sad and suffering." While not condemning announcement of a fast, Jesus reminds us not to flaunt our fasting in order to impress people.

Not everyone should fast. While stressing moderation, Babb warns that some should not attempt food fasts—pregnant or nursing women, anyone with present or past eating disorders, diabetics or people with kidney disease, those who must take medication with food, the frail elderly, or children (who may choose to avoid sugar or a favorite toy for a time).

Balance fasting and feasting. Babb points out that Sabbath and fasting have similarities, affirming that rhythms matter, providing structure for setting aside one thing to embrace another. They address different needs and compulsions. "The sabbath [*sic*] encourages us to face our addiction to being productive, our need to justify ourselves by what we do" . . . and "teaches grace at a deep and heartfelt place inside us. Because we stop many of our activities on the sabbath [*sic*], we learn that God loves us apart from what we do" (p. 138).

Why try fasting? Babb quotes John S. Mogabgab: " 'Can we hunger for Christ, the Bread of Life, when we are full of dishes enticingly served up on the steam table of a prosperous consumer culture? From what do we need to fast today so we may develop strength of soul tomorrow?' " (p. 108).

Young Men See Visions; Old Men Draw Maps

Recently I experienced a *déjà vu* moment when my colleague's father-in-law carefully detailed driving instructions for an oft-traveled route. When the old man finished, my colleague whispered, "Watch! He will instruct us again before we leave."

Sure enough, once we were in the car, ready to depart, the same excruciating details were repeated. The scenario recalled memories of my own father's little maps that he repetitiously thrust into his sons' hands to instruct us how to drive—even the familiar route back home. My colleague understood this preoccupation of old men—drawing maps to assure themselves that those who come afterward will find their way home safely.

The Old Testament provides just such a map. We view the book of Joshua as a dynamic story of mighty deliverance, powerful acts, and conquering glory. Of course, Joshua is all this and more. But remember, this narrative is first a historical record of what had already occurred.

You probably picture Joshua as the strong warrior who assisted Moses, spied out the land, stood for justice, led Israel across the Jordan River, and conquered Jericho. I easily imagine Joshua in his prime, maybe forty years of age. But Joshua was a senior citizen when Moses died. His spying partner, Caleb, already had reached eighty-five years of age. So when I heard Pastor Guideo Quinteros, president of the Seventh-day Adventist Church in Chile, preach these points from Joshua's account, I recognized that he was bringing to mind a road map for faithfulness.

God spoke to Joshua (Joshua 1:1). God enjoys speaking to His leaders today just as He spoke with Joshua. Thus, prayer is not only pouring our petitions into God's ear but also hearing His voice speak to our mind and heart. How shall we respond? Listen! God instructed Joshua (Joshua 1:2, NKJV). "Go over this Jordan, you and all this people." God's distinct purpose for His people—"You are here. I want you there!" Following God's instructions propels people into the Promised Land. How shall we respond? Move!

God promised success (Joshua 1:3, 5). "You will possess the land where you make your stand; no one will dare confront you." Leaders who follow God's direction are imbued with heavenly power. Neither human nor demonic forces will attain advantage when your dream matches God's dream and you follow His instructions. How shall we respond? Venture!

God called Joshua to strength and courage (Joshua 1:6, 7b). "Don't waver;

remain in the center; turning neither to extremes of left or right." Leaders cannot halt between two opinions. They must stand for something, or they will fall for anything. Endeavor boldly! How shall we respond? Achieve!

God expected sanctified people to anticipate great wonders (Joshua 3:5). When the Holy Spirit moves, people are called to holy living. A living, experiential, experimental faith takes God's word seriously, envisions victory, and lives in eager anticipation of God's faithfulness to accomplish what He has promised.

How shall we respond? Expect! God assured He would expand Joshua's influence (Joshua 3:7). "I will help you do great things. I will bring you good success. I will increase your ministry to the extent you permit me to increase your vision. You can trust your reputation to my strength." How shall we respond? Dream! God prepared His ministers for success: " 'Command the priests . . . , "stand in the Jordan" ' " (Joshua 3:8, NKJV). Take the leadership initiative. Nothing miraculous occurred until the leaders stepped into the water. There is a time to wait on the Lord and there is a time when pastors must move, step up to the challenge, and walk in anticipation of God's deliverance. How shall we respond? Lead! God commanded His people to memorialize His power (Joshua 4:7). Once they had crossed the Jordan River, Israel still faced great challenges and great opportunities: cities to fall, enemies to drive out, and continuing spiritual renewal and reform. First, however, Israel needed to memorialize God's mighty works. So mighty men transported huge stones from the riverbed to establish a memorial where future generations would pause, worship, and remember. For this same purpose Jesus created the Sabbath—a holy seventh of each week in which God's people pause, worship, and recall His providences. How shall we respond? Remember! How do we remember? Remember that Jesus made us and not we ourselves. Remember we are the work of God's hand and the sheep of His pasture. Remember we are the bride of His second coming, His chosen ones, His special people, His royal priesthood, His beloved. Remember God never abandons His own. Remember His plan. Remember His will. Remember His map!

Young men dream dreams. Old men draw maps. How shall we respond? Follow the map! Get ready. Get going. Get home safe. Choose ye this day. Choose life. Choose Jesus!

The Miracle of Working God's Way

An illustrated Bible story caught my attention. The artist had taken dramatic license in the rendition of a hatchet that had sprouted hands and feet with little fins—the swimming ax head.

Subsequently, I've discovered this story is much more instructive of God's leadership principles than mere entertainment.

Define your need. "And the sons of the prophets said to Elisha, 'See now, the place where we dwell with you is too small for us' " (2 Kings 6:1, NKJV). The need was self-evident—"this place is too small." They had insufficient room for their expanding group. Analysis of current reality is essential, for you cannot possibly go where you would like until you thoroughly understand where you are. Evaluate your situation until the need becomes self-evident to the majority of your team.

Design your plan. "Please, let us go to the Jordan, and let every man take a beam from there, and let us make there a place where we may dwell" (verse 2, NKJV). The young men brought Elisha a clear, detailed plan. A site had been selected, necessary resources had been identified and located, and a strategy had been developed for everyone's task. With planning considered essential, the more detail available the better. To develop ownership, the planning process becomes even more important than the final draft.

Defer to God's will. "So he answered, 'Go' " (verse 2, NKJV). With God's endorsement, success was guaranteed. When you advance, certain that you are following Heaven's will, you have the assurance of success. Scripture says, "We should make plans—counting on God to direct us" (Proverbs 16:9, TLB). You will discover no better basis for moving forward than assurance of God's approval. Prayerfully await God's permission. Then boldly venture where you otherwise would fear to go.

Determine your support. " 'Please consent to go with your servants.' And he answered, 'I will go' " (2 Kings 6:3, NKJV). When you have carefully designed your plan and prayerfully deferred to God's will, you are ready to enlist the support of others. Recruit your team. Seek counsel from your leaders and request their active participation. Your efforts, combined with Heaven's approval and your leaders' involvement, guarantee success.

Direct your actions. "So he went with them. And when they came to the Jordan, they cut down trees" (verse 4, NKJV). What a prescription for success: careful preparation immediately followed by diligent work—vision transformed into activity. Israel had previously been to Jordan but hesitated to cross into the Promised Land. They had set up camp and even held a prayer meeting, but nothing happened until the spiritual leaders moved the people forward. Once you have made your plan and sought God's will, go to work! Seize the initiative. Be about your duty.

Describe your trauma. "But as one was cutting down a tree, the iron ax head fell into the water; and he cried out and said, 'Alas, master! For it was borrowed' " (verse 5, NKJV). Even a God-endorsed project does not eliminate difficulties. In this life the reality of tragedy will repeatedly focus our attention on the wider view of God's promised new creation. If we could achieve a trouble-free existence here, we would not long for the blessed hope. However, differentiate between tragedy and trauma. This was not a tragic loss of life or serious injury. The trauma was loss of a borrowed tool by an embarrassed student loath to face the owner. Help your people understand God's interest in our concerns, large and small.

Delight in your miracles. "So the man of God said, 'Where did it fall?' . . . and he made the iron float" (verse 6, NKJV). Imagine the young man's relief. I'm certain there was rejoicing by the Jordan and I'm certain the story was retold hundreds of times by those who witnessed the event. Miracles generate ongoing testimonies of what wonderful things God has done. Sharing the story multiplies the powerful reassurance that if God is with us, who can be against us!

Designate your responsibility. "Pick it up for yourself" (verse 7, NKJV). Our response to a miracle means acting upon God's providence. The ax head floated, it did not swim to shore and jump up on the bank. Elisha's instructions were clear, "Pick it up for yourself!" Do what you can do. When God does His part, we must do our part. Cooperation with providential opportunities guarantees ultimate victory. When Jesus sent Peter fishing for Caesar's tax, the coin was already in the mouth of the fish. But the miracle was only accomplished when Peter followed instructions.

Decide to obey. "So he reached out his hand and took it" (verse 7, NKJV). Each of us has a choice. Obedience is a decision. The student could have observed the floating ax head and never retrieved the miracle. He could have heard the instructions but refused to participate. When God opens an opportunity, we must cooperate. When we decide to obey, miracles move from possibility to reality.

This powerfully illustrates the miracle of working God's way!

Believers Behaving Badly—
Part 1

Charles Bradford sums it up succinctly and poetically: *To live above with the saints in love, For me that will be glory! But to live below with the saints I know, That's another story!*

Beware any disconnect between belief and behavior. The path is wide, and the trap is easy to assume that good goals justify either suspect means or mean suspects.

Curious as it may sound to orthodoxy-loving minds, Jesus bases judgment not on our doctrines but on our behavior toward Him and the least of His brothers. That's right! While Jesus loves and upholds the truth—Himself being truth personified—He demands that truth be spoken in love. Should we fail this test, then any truth telling becomes merely clanging brass. Our worst behavior can occur at the very moment we mistakenly believe we are performing our best service. For example:

Abuse of platform. At a General Conference session some individuals, while standing at the microphones, railed as they urged evicting miscreants from membership for offenses ranging from tobacco usage to divorce.

Although the letter of law might permit such punishments, their opinions were recorded and published in such manner that brought more harm than good.

One individual, who had recently begun attending worship services in a distant location, read these "opinions" in the printed minutes and concluded that such harshness was the church's official position, rather than just the free expression of a delegate with a bad attitude.

Of course, no harm was intended by the publishers of the record, but clearly these diatribes, expressed with much less charity than Christ's love demands, were more than a new believer was able to bear and discouraged a "little one" at the very moment he should have been protected and nurtured, not lambasted.

Jesus uses the strongest warnings possible against those who would discourage "little ones" or new believers (Luke 17:1, 2). In fact, on the very topic of tobacco usage as reason for church action, I'm reminded of good counsel on how to deal with errant members.

> The course pursued toward Doctor Osborn has been all wrong.
> Had this man been handled judiciously he would have been a

blessing to the church. He has used tobacco to a greater or less degree, but this habit was not as offensive in the sight of God as the defects in the character of those who might judge him, for God weighs the motives. . . .

His human nature could not bear the unintelligent, unreasonable, unchristian, course pursued by men and women who had more zeal than knowledge. God has been displeased with, and dishonored by, them. . . .

Some have taken a position that those who use tobacco should be dealt with and turned out of the church. In all of our experience for many years not a case of this kind has thus been treated by us. We have borne with them and labored with and prayed with them for years, and if after a time, they did not reform they became lax in other things, and causes of a grievous character occurred which required an action on the part of the church. But then the responsibility was not assumed by merely the resident elder, the deacon, or any church member, but the church waited in patience for help, for wise counselors, and then moved with the greatest caution. These hasty movements in such cases tend to ruin a church. It shows a self-sufficient, self-important, bigoted spirit which if indulged will ruin any church. . . .

Doctor Osborn has not pursued that meek and Christian course which the Bible requires, but those who have condemned him have pursued a course far more objectionable in the sight of God than that pursued by him, and they are answerable for their influence. . . .

I was shown that the same injudicious treatment has been exercised toward others. Some precious souls that could not justify the unchristian course pursued toward the doctor were crowded until they have separated from the church, and others have been cut off. Such a spirit has taken possession of those who have ever carried things by storm that Satan, instead of the Spirit of Christ, has triumphed. Some of those who have been deprived of the fellowship of the church have been more worthy of a place in the church than those by whom they were cut off. God calls upon these to repent, and learn of Christ in the spirit of meekness, of self-denial, and love (Ellen G. White, *Manuscript Releases,* vol. 12, 285–287).

Of course, other examples abound of believers behaving badly that we will later discuss: abuse of knowledge, abuse of position, abuse of advantage, abuse of legality, and abuse of influence.

For the moment, however, let's strive to live in peace with the saints below if we expect ever to live with them in love above.

Believers Behaving Badly—
Part 2

In part 1, we bemoaned our tendency to disconnect belief from behavior, noting that some of our worst moments as believers occur when we mistakenly believe we are performing our best service.

Our orthodoxy (correct belief) is only as valuable as our orthopraxy (correct behavior). Remember, Jesus' description of the judgment (Matthew 25) rejects many outwardly orthodox believers.

In addition to "abuse of platform," in which we noted how some misguided believers think that publicly broadcasting their opinion guarantees virtue regardless of their behavior, other types of believers also behave badly.

Abuse of advantage. The note that the church organist delivered delineated her demands in a "take no hostages" stance that could have tutored a terrorist. "I'd rather that kid not come to church than to endure another instance of today's trashy music. If you permit a repeat, I'll leave this church and never return. What will you do then?"

In fairness to the organist's outrage, the youngster who had assaulted the special music was untrained, unkempt, and unaccomplished. The choice of music was poor and the delivery was worse. The only positive aspect I could muster from the whole ordeal was that the youngster's parents, rarely in attendance, were both present and blessed by their child's participation.

From a pastor's perspective, enduring a less than satisfactory rendition was compensated by the whole family having worshiped and the youngster having felt good about making a contribution to the service.

True to her threats, our organist marched her outstanding talents to another congregation, which she also held hostage to her own superior musical training and taste. Of course, we suffered from her loss, but we gained a number of families who were grateful that their mediocre talents now had opportunity for worship participation.

Abuse of position. Then there was the administrator who commanded compliance with his personal counterinterpretation of policy procedures. When a subordinate leader demurred, citing page and paragraph of established denominational policy, discussion turned to demand and the administrator threatened revenge at the next constituency nominating committee.

Phrases such as "I am in charge," "You don't comprehend authority," and "Because I said so" did little to change either mind while the role of the leader was belittled to that of a bully.

Abuse of influence. "Kick him out," an elder demanded of the church board about a relatively new member (carefully distinguish this designation from "relative church member," whom almost no church board will discipline, regardless of infraction), who had been spotted using tobacco just a few weeks after baptism. As the board was about to vote, another elder requested a delay. "Please, permit me time to get close to this individual. I'm a former smoker myself, and I'm embarrassed that none of us have become close to this new member. I would like to help."

Within a couple of months, our church had three new converts—the smoker who had reformed, the helping elder who learned to mentor new believers, and even the elder who had previously rushed to removal.

We began stop-smoking clinics, offered Alcoholics Anonymous in our facility, and started new small-group ministries for those who needed fellowship in other twelve-step programs.

Abuse of knowledge. Imagine the tragedy if that one leader's abuse of influence had not been countermanded by the elder who determined to aid a weaker brother! And speaking of such, I'm neither impressed nor intimidated by those who demand compliance by resorting to misinterpretation of "weaker brother" terminology.

If I have sufficient knowledge to make the claim for myself, I am ineligible for the appellation. Superior knowledge that claims spurious position as "weaker brother" removes me from such status and places me in need of a constant reminder of Jesus' story about the prodigal's "stronger sibling."

Abuse of legality. Jesus constantly strove to distinguish between law's demands and love's constraints without compromising either.

For example, Jesus validated legal technicalities concerning divorce while narrowing the terminology of sufficient grounds. He said, "because of your hard hearts, Moses permitted you to divorce, but I affirm that even if you lust in your heart, you have committed adultery" (cf. Matthew 19:8; 5:28).

Likewise, Jesus never compromised the claims of justice while He encouraged ongoing virtue in new life. He told badly behaving believers, "If you are without sin, cast the first stone to implement the deserved death penalty." But to the guilty sinner, he affirmed, "I do not condemn you, go and sin no more!" (cf. John 8:7, 11).

Now that's a believer behaving boldly!

What My Psychiatrist Didn't Tell Me

Soon after the death of my brother and four other colleagues in a tragic plane crash, I began seeing a psychiatrist to help me process the awesome loss and overwhelming pain.

Friends and colleagues, as well as countless acquaintances, offered sympathy and expressed condolences, but as the weeks continued, I knew that I needed qualified professional counseling. First I made an appointment every week. Now I see him monthly, which seems about right for me as I approach the one-year anniversary.

I have never kept my visits a secret and several friends, especially those who know my lifelong fear of flying, have asked, "What does your psychiatrist tell you?" As I've responded to their queries and pondered my own experience, I have concluded that greater discoveries have come from things my psychiatrist has not told me than from the things he has said. For example:

My psychiatrist never told me, "You're crazy." In fact, one of the sanest things I have ever done was to recognize a challenge beyond my normal coping skills and to sense my urgent need for a listening/engaging voice beyond my own devotional life. While I remain a firm believer in the therapeutic value of prayer to heal and restore, I also recognize that some challenges may need in-depth conversation, probing reflection and feedback coupled with penetrating questioning and demanding account ability. For me, this very process has been the product. By regularly encountering a professional who prods my thinking and challenges my emotional responses, I am experiencing the therapeutic product for which I sought professional care.

By the way, if it brings any consolation to those who wonder, he has never told me that I am "not crazy." So since I don't possess certification either way, you are welcome to your own opinion.

My psychiatrist never told me, "This is not real." At no point in this process has the tragic event which broke into our family been minimized. Our loss was sudden, devastating, public, and drastic for a much wider circle of individuals than our initial ability to grasp.

In the midst of our trauma, strangers were kind beyond measure and well intentioned "friends of Job" were cruel beyond comprehension as they, too, reacted to circumstances which never could have been foreseen, much less controlled, and only can be endured. Selfish graspings collided with selfless acts of gracious mercy to make harsh reality simultaneously harder to bear and easier to survive.

My psychiatrist has never suggested that my grief, which has ranged the full gamut of typical emotions, was not normal, or to be expected, or to be experienced. Beyond an occasional-use sleeping aid, he has not offered, nor have I felt I needed, medication. However, should my feelings of loss expand into insurmountable emotional hopelessness, it would be appropriate and necessary to consider a prescription for clinical depression.

My psychiatrist never told me, "Everything will be OK." Not once has he suggested that everything I am experiencing will turn out all right. He has never denied, nor encouraged me to deny, the long-term consequences for Dave's widowed spouse, his orphaned daughter, our aged and shattered parent, or the grieving team in his conference. Awesome consequences whether emotional, financial, organizational, or familial will continue into the unforeseeable distance. There is no morning in which I will ever awaken suddenly to discover "it is all over." I cannot tell you what will trigger the next pain wave nor can I predict when I will ever have one full day in which I don't reach for the phone to share some funny incident with my brother who can never answer my ring. Reality is harsh and permanent.

Finally, my psychiatrist never told me, "Something better is coming." With some admitted amazement on his part, my psychiatrist has probed my faith and absolute confidence that I will see Dave again. He questions why I don't pray for my brother's soul which I know is at rest, and why I don't worry about his eventual salvation which I know is secure. I cannot imagine how anyone without such assurance could withstand grief's onslaught.

But, to borrow the words of a colleague who recently wrote, "Dave and I spent so much time sharing with each other about work, our marriages, emotions, college football, the foibles (as you describe them), our demons and our delights . . . that it has left me somewhat disoriented for all that to have abruptly ended without my permission. Kinda like calling a play at the scrimmage line, dropping back to pass, then realizing all your receivers have disappeared. I just keep telling myself, 'Man, you were born into a world at war and bad things happen in war. Soldiers get wounded, maimed, killed. When the war's over, the regiment will be reunited.' "

Even so, come, Lord Jesus!

How Would I Know?

In all my years of writing, I've never received as many significant responses to anything as the previous article, "What My Psychiatrist Didn't Tell Me," which I published in my monthly column for the *Ministry* magazine. Most of the interactions came "below the radar" in the form of affirmation, comments, questions, dialogue, and a couple severe criticisms that I would admit to seeing a therapist or that the denomination would permit me to reveal such a horrible and secret shame.

However, behind most of the feedback and questions has been the recurring query, How would someone know if they needed to see a professional therapist? Typically this question has been preceded by, "Of course, I haven't experienced a tragedy like your sudden loss of your brother and friends in a plane crash, but . . ."

I have decided to return to this subject for precisely the reasons that seem to lie behind these questions. How does someone know when they need help beyond their spouse, their friends, their church family, and their personal prayer and devotional life?

Have we attached so much shame and prohibition to the process of seeking counsel that real needs are not being addressed and pastoral caregivers are attempting to help individuals even as they remain deeply wounded and untreated themselves?

In "Pastor, Deal With Your 'Soul Holes,' "[1] an anonymously written article, a minister of more than two decades describes confronting his own traumas while serving as a pastoral counselor during the aftermath of the Oklahoma City bombings. "After each meeting, the care teams were required to debrief with a psychologist. I remember thinking, *What a waste of time to debrief with this shrink. I'm around death and dying frequently as a pastor. I don't need debriefing.*"

He continues, "After all, we pastors have to be tough. Pain, sorrow, trauma, and conflict are commonplace in our lives. Nothing sticks to our Teflon hearts. I'd referred a boatload of neurotic parishioners to psychologists over the years, but I didn't need one. I was a counselor . . . But after nearly a quarter century of church work, I began to see my own need for therapy. For years I'd wrestled with free-floating anger, which would pop up as irritability, defensiveness, a need 'to win,' sarcasm, condescending speech, restlessness, and other symptoms."

---

1. "Pastor, Deal With Your 'Soul Holes,' " *Rev! Magazine,* January-February 2006, 134.

A sidebar to this penetrating article lists seven signs, any one of which may indicate the need to talk to a reputable, professional counselor to discover if inner issues might be holding you back in your ministry's effectiveness:

1. You have frequent, low-grade anger and/or feel defensive and irritable.
2. You feel depressed about ministry and life and/or experience mood swings.
3. You wrestle with addictive behaviors: alcohol, drugs, sex, or others.
4. You pursue workaholism, justifying it out of need or ambition.
5. You recognize traumatic events in your past, but you've never discussed them openly with a counselor.
6. You're in frequent conflict with others at home and at work.
7. You have marital or parenting problems that don't go away. When others mention them, you dismiss the topic or the person.

Noting the intimate connection between our mental and physical health, Ellen White stated, "The relation that exists between the mind and the body is very intimate. When one is affected, the other sympathizes. The condition of the mind affects the health to a far greater degree than many realize. Many of the diseases from which men suffer are the result of mental depression. Grief, anxiety, discontent, remorse, guilt, distrust, all tend to break down the life forces and to invite decay and death."[2]

Our anonymous pastoral writer continues (and perhaps his choice to remain anonymous says something significant about the scope of this challenge), "Pride kept me from seeking help in those times when I wondered if I might benefit from the perspectives of a trained professional. My roles as a 'tough' pastor and a Bible know-it-all made it even more difficult for me to admit my need for help."

In his conclusion, "Embracing My Weaknesses," he says, "Paul's writing to the Corinthians has come to make more sense than ever: *So now* I am glad to boast about *my weaknesses, so that the power of Christ can work through me. That's why I take pleasure in my weaknesses, and in the insults, hardships, persecutions, and troubles that I suffer for Christ. For when I am weak, then I am strong* (2 Cor. 12:9, 10, emphasis added). I used to think that health was a matter of embracing my strengths and pretending I had no significant soul holes. I've come to realize that only when I'm willing and able to embrace my weaknesses as well as strengths can I ever hope to become healthy."

I've concluded that the strongest thing we can do is to get the help we need.

_____

2. Ellen G. White, *The Ministry of Healing* (Mountain View, Calif.: Pacific Press® Publishing Association, 1942), 241.

Leadership During the Delay

Leaders demonstrate their character more clearly in adversity than in prosperity. Contrast the vacillation of Aaron with the faithfulness of Moses during Israel's delayed expectations.

"When Moses failed to come back down the mountain right away, the people went to Aaron. 'Look,' they said, 'make us some gods who can lead us. This man Moses, who brought us here from Egypt, has disappeared. We don't know what has happened to him' " (Exodus 32:1, NLT).

Fed up with waiting, the people demanded immediate action. Moses was out of sight and they were out of faith. Unfortunately, when he should have stood strong, Aaron caved to their demands for visible, multiple gods and collected their offerings.

"Then Aaron took the gold, melted it down, and molded and tooled it into the shape of a calf. The people exclaimed, 'O Israel, these are the gods who brought you out of Egypt!' " (verse 4, NLT). Although he would later claim that a miraculous occurrence produced the golden calf, Scripture describes Aaron actively fashioning the idol and, subsequently, leading the congregation in false worship.

"When Aaron saw how excited the people were about it, he built an altar in front of the calf and announced, 'Tomorrow there will be a festival to the Lord!' So the people got up early the next morning to sacrifice. . . . After this, they celebrated with feasting and drinking, and indulged themselves in pagan revelry" (verses 5, 6, NLT).

Heaven, however, was not caught unaware by their rebellion.

"Then the Lord told Moses, 'Quick! Go down the mountain! The people you brought from Egypt have defiled themselves. They have already turned from the way I commanded them to live. They have made an idol shaped like a calf, and they have worshiped and sacrificed to it. They are saying, "These are your gods, O Israel, who brought you out of Egypt." ' Then the Lord said, 'I have seen how stubborn and rebellious these people are. Now leave me alone so my anger can blaze against them and destroy them all. Then I will make you, Moses, into a great nation instead of them' " (verses 7–10, NLT).

The wages of sin is death, and God was fully prepared to penalize Israel for their rebellion, a sin He declares equal to witchcraft. But as a true pastor, Moses began to intercede, asking that his own life be cut off if God could not spare the people. Moses even urged God's own reputation as a reason to spare the people. "But Moses pleaded with the LORD his God not to do it. . . . 'The Egyptians will say, "God tricked them into coming to the mountains so he could kill them and wipe them from the face of the earth." Turn away from your fierce anger. Change your mind about this terrible disaster you are planning against your people! Remember your covenant. . . .' So the LORD withdrew His threat" (verses 11–14, NLT).

Just as God had previously responded to Abraham's entreaties for Sodom, He now extended mercy in response to Moses' plea. Mercy did not avert judgment, however. "Moses saw the calf and the dancing. In terrible anger, he threw the stone tablets to the ground, smashing them at the foot of the mountain. He took the calf they had made and melted it in the fire. And when the metal had cooled, he ground it into powder and mixed it with water. Then he made the people drink it" (verses 19, 20, NLT).

Notice their radically different leadership styles as Moses demands accountability from Aaron, who attempts to shift the blame for his own behavior to the people. " 'What did the people do to you?' he demanded. 'How did they ever make you bring such terrible sin upon them?' " (verse 21, NLT).

" 'Don't get upset, sir,' Aaron replied. 'You yourself know these people and what a wicked bunch they are. They said to me, "Make us some gods to lead us, for something has happened to this man Moses, who led us out of Egypt." So I told them, "Bring me your gold earrings." When they brought them to me, I threw them into the fire—and out came this calf!' " (verses 22–24, NLT). Imagine! Aaron's apostasy is so bound up with the rebellion that he declares his own efforts (the basis of every false religion is salvation by works) to be a miraculous consequence.

Aaron's failure in leadership, coupled with the nation's rebellion, demanded a call for repentance and reformation, especially in light of the scandal their behavior had brought upon God's name and reputation in full view of nonbelieving enemies. So Moses confronted the issue directly.

"When Moses saw that Aaron had let the people get completely out of control—and much to the amusement of their enemies—he stood at the entrance to the camp and shouted, 'All of you who are on the LORD's side, come over here and join me.' And all the Levites came" (verses 25, 26, NLT).

Today, when our Lord's return appears delayed, God still seeks leaders who will discern the truth, stand for right, and call for radical faithfulness to God's plan. How will you and I lead?

Don't Miss the Boat

Nearly twenty-five years ago, I doubled my one fine-art print of Edward Hicks's *Noah's Ark* with a second ark. I inadvertently began a collection that, had I realized its ultimate size, I might never have chosen to expand.

Today, guests who tour the General Conference headquarters enjoy viewing my display, which ranges from the remarkable and valuable to the truly kitschy. My collection grows by the well-intentioned generosity of those who ship items often addressed only to the one who collects Noah's Arks.

For a number of months now, I've received numerous copies of a cartoon illustrating a woodpecker drilling a hole in the ark, accompanied by proverbial truisms which may have some spiritual value for pastors:

Don't miss the boat. Priorities are essential. Many urgent matters can preoccupy our attention as well as our activities, but above all else, we must prioritize the things Jesus prioritizes to prepare ourselves and our people for His return. How tragic to miss the boat!

Remember, we are all in the same boat. Often it seems easier to compete than to cooperate. Our too-easily-adopted attitudes of "us versus them" can destroy our individual influence as well as our corporate impact.

Plan ahead. It wasn't raining when Noah built the ark. If heaven's first rule is "order," then planning becomes essential, whether long range for the growth of the church or shorter range for sermons and worship services. Dwight D. Eisenhower said it well, "Planning is everything; plans are nothing." The very process of planning engages the creative spirit as well as the cooperation of those whose teamwork is needed for success.

The woodpecker may have to go. Refuse to permit a few negative complainers to hold your congregation or your goals hostage by their repetitive drilling. Usually the vast majority is with you, and if your leaders concur with your vision, you are safe to ignore the vocal minority.

Stay fit. When you're sixty years old, someone may ask you to do something really big. Our youth-saturated society needs ministries to children and youth, especially the essential task of deploying them in service for the Master. Equally important, we must honor, value, and utilize the contribution of seniors whose time and talents sustain multiplied church programs.

Don't listen to critics; just get on with the job. If you allow skeptics and scoffers to set your agenda, little or nothing of import will be accomplished. If, like Nehemiah, you are too preoccupied with important matters to sink to their level, these barking dogs will eventually tire of their own noise and retreat or, better yet, join the mission. Don't stoop to the level of your critics. Never wrestle with a pig. You cannot win and the pig enjoys the fight.

Build your future on high ground. Focus on eternity. Relegate low-value issues to the level of their ultimate impact. For example, don't bog down fighting over carpet colors when weightier matters are neglected. Likewise for interpersonal relationships. Thinking leaders talk about ideas and observe people. Reactionaries talk about people and only observe ideas.

For safety's sake, travel in pairs. Team ministry is Jesus' plan. Work two-by-two for specific reasons such as safety (both of your person and your reputation) and success (two are more effective than one; plus each learns from the other). Try to include your spouse in partnership as the modern fulfillment of our Lord's design.

Speed isn't always an advantage. The snails were on board with the cheetahs. The more worthy a project, the more time it may take to fulfillment. Get started. Making progress may be more important than completion. Faithfulness is measured by consistency.

When stressed, float awhile. If you cannot remember your last vacation, then you have not taken sufficient time off. Frenetic activity is no indication of either importance or wisdom. No pastor has ever been busier than Jesus, who regularly found time for spiritual, social, and recreational retreats. Take your days off. Even if you believe you don't need them, your spouse and your members know that you do!

The ark was built by amateurs; the Titanic *by professionals.* However, the ark's design specifications were from God. Nothing can limit the effectiveness of amateurs as long as they follow Heaven's plan.

No matter the storm, when you are with God, there's always a rainbow waiting. In this life, God's people will experience trials. A better world is coming. His kingdom is just around the corner. Even during your lonely times, remember Jesus' promise, "I will see you again"! (John 16:22, NKJV).

If tempted to despair, refocus. The only thing that made life tolerable on board that ark full of smelly animals was the sure and certain knowledge that things were a whole lot worse on the outside. If circumstances seem overwhelming and your problems multiply, just remind yourself of how much worse things are outside.

Above all, when you hear God's invitation, don't miss the boat!

Pray for Rain

Scripture compares the outpouring of the Holy Spirit to rain; special, abundant quantities of the Spirit preparing the soil for harvest. Consider dedicating a month to leading your congregations in special prayer—thirty-one specific topics; one for each day of the month.

It is time to pray! Be specific, timely, and inclusive. Pray for . . .

1. *Yourself, your spouse, your children.* Determine to rededicate your life and ministry to Jesus; making His priorities your priorities. Satan will do everything possible to destroy your marriage or to weaken its joy. Begin with apology, if needed, and affirmation that is always welcome. Ask the Holy Spirit to help you sensitively minister to "your first mission field."

2. *Peace.* We worship the Prince of Peace. Pray for goodwill to flourish. "Let there be peace on earth; and let it begin with me."

3. *Unity.* On the night of His betrayal, unity of His believers was the focus of Jesus' prayer. His desire still echoes: "that they might be one!"

4. *New believers.* Jesus prayed for those who would believe through the preaching of His disciples. Jesus understands that new believers must be surrounded by love and fortified by prayer.

5. *Your preaching.* Ask the Spirit to help you provide the best spiritual menu. Planning your sermons a year ahead enables the Holy Spirit to direct your thinking along the plan you have established.

6. *The lost.* Praying for lost souls does not change God's mind about their condition or make Heaven more willing to save. Praying for the lost changes *your mind* as you begin to see the lost through Heaven's eyes.

7. *Change.* Something must become different. Insanity believes we can continually repeat the past, yet experience different results. Ask for a burst of holy creativity.

8. *Singles.* Thousands of unmarrieds, many of them young professionals, become isolated from the church when they experience only couple-oriented messages. Seek to involve every "one" in church life.

9. *Disgruntled.* Almost every congregation harbors unhappy critics focusing on traumas, alarmism, extremist views, and peripheral

35

agendas. These well-intentioned dragons cause havoc, especially when their venom combines with peculiar heresies or when they major in minors. Pray that they will convert or leave.

10. *Public servants.* Your community depends upon police, firefighters, teachers, hospital administrators, emergency technicians, and countless others who maintain necessary services. Pray for these "ministers" and honor them in your worship services.

11. *Pray-ers.* Ask the Lord for prayer warriors who will focus on your church, lead the spiritual battle against evil, and encourage those needing specific, intercessory prayer. Remember, "prayer does not change things; prayer changes people!"

12. *Prodigals.* Virtually every family could list those who have journeyed far, even if they have never left home. Ask Heaven to make your life a witness to welcome them back.

13. *Neighbors.* On our streets live divorced/single parents, overworked and overstressed young adults alongside retirees, gays, and secularists next to those from the religious right, as well as gracious neighbors from various national, racial, and religious heritages. Pray they will consider Jesus as a result of living near us.

14. *Givers.* Rather than bemoaning traumatic consequences of global recession, seek thousands to come to Jesus who will bring the treasure of their hearts along with the treasure in their pockets. Design ministries to captivate commitment so their hearts will follow their treasure into God's mission.

15. *Women leaders.* Seek to deploy this 70 percent of our members. Emphasize the power of women's evangelistic witness (the Samaritan woman's revival, Mary's personal resurrection testimony, Priscilla's instructing influence, and Phoebe's congregational leadership). When you have employment opportunities, consider a woman.

16. *Unloved saved ones.* Every congregation has faithful individuals who rarely experience any expression of love. Organize your members to invite others into their homes and fellowship circles. They might entertain angels!

17. *Hope.* Imagine the audacity of hope to believe this world can move beyond national, racial, class, and social warfare. Jesus guarantees this when He returns—the Blessed Hope. Jesus can begin it now in your congregation—Blessed Assurance!

18. *War.* Pray for combatants on both sides of conflict. Pray for their spouses, children, and parents. Encourage chaplains and congregations who minister to military forces.

19. *Discernment.* Scripture invites you to pray for wisdom that you lack. God's Word, the Holy Spirit, and Christ's body—the church—will guide you to discover His will.

20. *National leaders.* Join me in praying for the president and for governmental leaders everywhere. "When we pray for God to change leaders, we affect them and everyone who follows them. Praying for our leaders results in an atmosphere conducive to the spreading of the gospel" (John C. Maxwell, *The Maxwell Leadership Bible,* Maxwell Motivation Publishers; see 1 Timothy 2:1–4).

21. *Revival.* Pray now for an abundant experience during the next Week of Prayer you will conduct. Plan, promote, prepare, and produce creative, participative services during that special week and watch the Spirit bless your efforts. Reform follows revival.

22. *Maturity.* Discipleship moves new believers beyond conversion to spiritual maturity. Jesus did not commission seeking for more entries, He envisioned more disciples. Any plans that separate evangelism from follow-up has schemed its own defeat.

23. *Holiness.* Spiritual disciplines should mark our lives. Pastoral responsibility includes specific guidance in those disciplines. Emphasize the ways to holiness—Bible study, prayer, fellowship, witnessing, and obedience. Sanctification accompanies those on this path.

24. *Teachers.* Adventists spend more denominational money on parochial education than all other ventures combined. Support the Lord's empowerment of our teachers as evangelists. Pray for all of our school teachers.

25. *Vision.* Consider big plans and bold ventures. Vision is different than sight. Mere sight surveys reality and wonders why things remain the same. Vision sees potential and claims the promise of power to achieve. Gather your leaders and brainstorm ideas that challenge.

26. *Colleagues.* Pastors of every denomination face daily challenges in shepherding the flocks that Christ has given them. Pray with and for ministers. Participate in your local Ministerial Association. Share professional development opportunities. Request their prayers for you: I ask you to pray for me.

27. *Elders.* These men and women are your own pastoral team to make the Lord's work effective in your church. Pray for and with them. Gather them often to seek Heaven's favor. Remember that healthcare administrators, literature evangelists, departmental leaders, and conference officials are integral teammates.

28. *Big cities.* Jesus loves people. People exist in cities. If you could effectively minister there, ask the Lord to deploy you where millions of residents need your spiritual influence. Flee to the cities to live godly lives in the ungodly environments.

29. *More workers.* Jesus never asked us to pray for the harvest. The harvest is ready! Thousands are on the verge of the kingdom, waiting to be gathered. Jesus commands us to pray the Lord of the harvest will send forth reapers.

30. *Love.* Do you want more effective outreach? The secret is simple—loving and lovable Christians. Friends win friends to Jesus. Ask the Savior to help you to love.

31. *The end.* Pray that Jesus comes soon. When I pastored, I preached the last week of every month on the Second Coming. Proclaim the Blessed Hope and you will discover your members keenly desiring the appearance of our Redeemer. Even so come, Lord Jesus!

More

The unreality of most resolutions is in direct proportion to their inherent inability to be kept—this year I will reduce my weight back to the thirty-two-inch waistline I enjoyed at age thirteen. Like Israel raising its collective hand to pledge "all that the Lord has said, we will do," our promises focus on the intent of our own efforts more than on our expectations for heaven's empowerment.

On the other hand, some resolutions not only are possible, they are essential for increased effectiveness in ministry. Relying on the Holy Spirit's power, I believe we can expect and experience more each year. Specifically . . .

More confidence. God is still on His throne and we can trust Him. We can even trust Him with our own experience of sanctification. "Being confident of this very thing, that He who has begun a good work in you will complete it until the day of Jesus Christ" (Philippians 1:6, NKJV).

More discernment. Too often, winds of unsound doctrine and tickling falsehoods fascinate our members and even captivate our preaching. Through the Holy Spirit's power, we can "measure twice and cut once" rather than advancing every whim and rumor.

More invitations. Extending gospel invitations is really a choice. If we conclude every message with a call to accept Jesus, results will multiply. Reject making calls only when you suppose someone is present who needs to make a decision but rather upon the reality that someone needs to decide upon that which you have preached with specific purpose. Otherwise, why did you preach? More growth. The fields are ripe, ready for harvest. Do not pray for greater results; pray for reapers.

More concern. Thousands attend worship services longing to hear some good news. They hunger and thirst to see Jesus and His righteousness and deserve our deep concern for their individual and corporate spiritual welfare. Pastor with compassion.

More quality. Clergy lead too many slap-dashed services which have been cobbled together in the vestry rather than planned and prayed into excellence. Even the holy angels cannot sustain interest in such lame offerings.

More opportunities. Too many pastors perform too much work themselves rather than recruiting, training, and deploying laity leaders. And too many ignore the available effective ministry leadership potential of our women and youth that comprise 70 percent of the membership.

More vision. Pray heaven to show you the possibilities beyond just next week's service or next month's paycheck. Pray and prepare for where God wants your congregation to be five new years from today.

More mission. And pray heaven to awaken a sense of global need; a view beyond your own precincts. The vitality of your local congregation will be directly impacted by the distance it can see and then participate in ministry beyond its own borders.

More tolerance. Remember, your way is not the only way. Familiarity does not guarantee success. Try new methods and respect those who may differ. While we need unity in doctrine, we desperately need tolerance for differing methodologies. Anyone who believes their mother is the best cook in the world has never traveled far.

More giving. Never apologize for asking people to give. Teach and preach stewardship—both systematic and project benevolence. The hearts of your members will end up in exactly the same place as their treasure.

More focus. You will never do everything you would like to accomplish. Success requires prioritizing. Know and understand your limitations and determine where to expend your energies. "This one thing I do" brings greater results than "These many things I intended!" More affirmation. Appreciation motivates those upon whom our success depends. Begin with your spouse and kids and move on to your elders, laity leaders, and school teachers. If you really want to stir things up, drop a Thank you note to your judicatory leaders.

More help. Your encouraging telephone call or thoughtful note may be just the lift a colleague needs to sustain burdens that seem overwhelming. If you think you ought to contact someone—you ought to! More reconciliation. Sometimes that note or telephone call needs to be an apology. Even attempting a restoration of fractured relationships eases your own soul and initiates a process that may produce healing later on.

More hope. Return again and again to the certainty of Jesus' promised return. Preaching the blessed hope both motivates and prepares your members. If you're ever in doubt as to what to say, preach the Second Coming.

More Jesus. Make our Lord the theme of every sermon, the center of every doctrine, the focus of every prayer, and the reason for every call.

And what will this produce?

More!

SECTION II:
REACHING HEARTS AND MINDS

Practical Prophecy

Along with several itinerating colleagues, I teach a Bible class at our local congregation. Teaching schedules are determined by which dates we can attend our home church. Imagine my concern when I was scheduled to teach the lesson on Daniel 2, a prophecy that I have preached many times, but also one that most of my class attendees would have often presented.

Searching for a fresh approach, I determined to present a verse-by-verse exegetical presentation of practical lessons that arise from the prophecy. Next time you are called upon to plow familiar furrows, try a fresh approach of asking what God says in the story behind the prophecy.

(Daniel 2:1) Pay attention to what keeps you awake. God may be trying to get a message through. He may use insomnia to arrest your mind.

(2) Desperate people will try anything. The magicians, astrologers, and sorcerers all proved to be charlatans.

(5) People will turn against those who deceive them. Never underestimate the wrath of those who have been deceived.

(12, 13) Good people get caught in the turmoil of the wicked. All will suffer the consequences of rebels.

(17, 18) Small groups have great power. When Daniel and his friends prayed, heaven moved!

(19, 20) God cares for His people. God does not act without revealing His secrets to His servants, the prophets.

(21–23) God remains in control. He sets up and takes down kings. His throne remains the constant of history. Never doubt His power to work in your own circumstances.

(24) Righteous believers spare the wicked. Just as God was willing to spare Sodom if a few righteous were found there, the lives of Babylonian soothsayers were spared because of Daniel and his friends.

(25) Some nonbelievers make correct judgment calls. Arioch acted quickly to resolve the death decree.

(26) Don't be intimidated by the skeptics. Nebuchadnezzar could hardly believe that a novice would provide answers that "wise men" had missed. He discovered that wise answers, indeed, can come from unexpected sources.

(28–30) Don't take credit for someone else's wisdom. Daniel was quick to credit the God of heaven as the source of all truth.

(31–35) Plainly proclaiming facts brings conviction to your listeners. The king

was so amazed by the truth that he never doubted the application.

(37, 38) Always begin with the good news. What despotic king could resist the appeal of "Thou art this head of gold" (KJV)? But keep everything in perspective. "For the God of heaven has given you a kingdom, power, strength, and glory" (NKJV).

(39) Watch your backside. Your downfall could come at the hands of a weaker force. Heaven sometimes uses inferiors to bring judgment.

(39) History demonstrates the reality of devolution. Humanity grows worse, not better. Just as silver is inferior to gold, brass to silver, and iron to brass, the natural order of a sinful world is progressive degeneration, not evolutionary progress.

(40–42) Historicism is proven by history. The historicist approach to understanding Bible prophecy has been validated by the flow of human history. God's Word can be trusted with the few prophecies yet unfilled.

(43) Iron and clay don't mix. The strength of iron is compromised by the fragility of ceramic pottery. Human efforts to forge strength from weak ingredients always fail.

(44) Kingdom-building belongs to God. Nebuchadnezzar as well as succeeding empires discovered that God has been setting up His kingdom—first His kingdom of grace; ultimately His kingdom of glory—"in the days of these kings" (NKJV). We live in history's latter days. Great prophetic waymarks have moved "past the kingdoms four, down to the feet—part of iron, part of clay, soon to pass away" (song written by Franklin Belden, 1886).

(45) The dream is certain; the interpretation is sure. Without help from human hands, God will set up His kingdom. His kingdom of glory is next! God's judgment, God's fiat creation, and God's permanence will stand. The conclusion is as certain and as sure as the original dream.

(46) Truth tellers are exalted. In a world engrossed with counterfeits and overwhelmed by falsehood, those who testify to truth will be rewarded.

(47ff) End with the good news. Prophetic messages lead to conversions. Understanding God's truth develops trust in His promises. Preach that the God who moves through history is still on His throne. With His plan, His promise, His providences secure, His return is as certain as the dawn!

Teaching That Transforms

Preaching that does not transform behavior has failed, whether we are preaching to our established members or to potential converts.

Mike Bellah says, "More than anything else, this generation needs biblical teaching. Our minds need to be renewed with expectations born not in the culture, but in the Word of God. . . Potential believers need to know that all truth is not relative, and experience is only one test of truth—often misleading in the short run."[1]

We are good at exposition, but are we as good at transformation? Far too often we assume that because something has been stated well, it has been thoroughly comprehended. This is not the case.

Repetitive instruction is essential. Michael Green argues that the instruction of new members through preaching must be more than just proclaiming truth. It must take root in the heart and be lived out in the life.

We tried to do this in a variety of ways. One was by having carefully planned courses of sermons: sometimes topical, sometimes following the church's year, sometimes expository. We tried to be sensitive to what the needs were at the time. Gradually we learned how foolish we were to dart from subject to subject each week. We needed to go on teaching on a particular topic until it is learned and acted upon. With this in mind, we organized a nine-month course, examining what it meant to be an alternative society in a world that is falling apart. We spent a whole month on each of nine aspects of this theme, and teaching took place at all levels in the church. The team preached on each topic for a whole month. The fellowship groups and prayer meetings discussed its application. Slide-tape sequences were produced for each topic. And we even made a loose-leaf guide book to the whole nine-month series, with opportunities for members to add materials of their own.[2]

Speaking specifically to grounding new believers into the church, Ellen White admonished Adventist preachers: "If those who knew the truth and were established in it were indeed in need of having its importance kept ever before them and their minds stirred up by the repetition of it, how important

---

1. Mike Bellah, *Baby Boom Believers* (Wheaton, Ill.: Tyndale House, 1973), 143.
2. Michael Green, *Freed to Serve: Training and Equipping for Ministry* (Dallas, Tex.: Word Publishing, 1983), 124.

that this work is not neglected for those newly come to the faith."[3]

Information, alone, is insufficient. However, a reliance on knowledge alone—conveying correct information into the comprehension of the new believer—may contribute to the church remaining a closed community more than we have realized. If we conclude that information alone disciples individuals, then we are in danger of spiritual haughtiness similar to that of the Corinthians who concluded that superior wisdom equaled superior spirituality.

I have known dozens within the church whose theological comprehension was accurate but whose lives did not reflect the life-changing differences the gospel expects. Clearly something was needed beyond accurate theology. They needed not only a knowledge of "the truth," they needed a personal relationship with Jesus Christ—*the Truth!*

Transformation is required by the gospel. Roger L. Dudley and Des Cummings say, "If we have nothing more than textual proofs for our distinctive beliefs, we will not begin to earn a hearing, for the world wants to know what meaning and relevance our message has for their lives."[4]

John R. W. Stott puts it well:

> In addition to integrity, our preaching of repentance and of Christ's lordship requires realism. It is not enough to call people to repentance in vague terms, as if conversion could take place in a kind of mystical vacuum out of which all real life has been sucked. When John the Baptist preached his baptism of repentance he insisted that people responding must "bear fruits that befit repentance." Nor did he leave it there. He went on to specific issues. The affluent must share their surplus wealth with the deprived. Tax collectors must replace extortion by probity. And soldiers must never use their power to rob people, but rather be content with their wages (Luke 3:8, 10-14). . . We need to spell out in realistic and concrete terms the contemporary implications of repentance, conversion, and the lordship of Jesus Christ.[5]

So what is the role of instruction for new converts and its relationship to assimilating the new believers into the life of the church? The answer is simple, yet direct and challenging. Our preaching must transform believers—whether established members or new converts—into worthy citizens of the church

3. Ellen G. White, *Evangelism* (Washington, D.C.: Review and Herald® Publishing Association, 1970), 334.

4. Roger L. Dudley and Des Cummings Jr., *Adventures in Church Growth* (Hagerstown, Md.: Review and Herald® Publishing Association, 1983), 33.

5. John R. W. Stott, *Christian Mission in the Modern World* (Downers Grove, Ill.: InterVarsity Press, 1975), 118.

(experiencing the fellowship of the saints), worthy citizens of society (living in the world as salt and light), and worthy citizens of the soon approaching kingdom (preparing to meet the Lord).

This is teaching that transforms.

Keeping the Commandments

We applaud the renewed interest in God's commandments as evidenced in events like the Ten Commandments Day. We commend the emphasis given to godly living, spiritual renewal, and the challenge of turning hearts and minds toward our eternal God and His unchanging law. As longtime advocates of a grace-motivated observance of the entire Decalogue by born-again Christians, Adventists can and should enthusiastically affirm those who are now standing up for God's law in the midst of a world that appears to ignore it.

This renewed emphasis on the moral law of God stands in welcome contrast to the messages all too frequently heard in some pulpits, messages that give distinct impressions that Christians can safely ignore the Ten Commandments because they have all been "nailed to the cross" and are no longer of importance to the followers of Jesus. At the same time, those of us who have labored in this field for some time can and should humbly offer a few crucial observations to this growing movement of sincere believers who share our deep concern for the role of faith and Christian influence in culture. What would Jesus do? is still the most helpful guideline as we communicate to our secular society the clear mandates of God's eternal law. All other observations grow out of this conviction.

Emulate rather than legislate. Jesus didn't lobby the Roman Senate for legislation requiring observance of the commandments by citizen and subject alike. And not because He believed the world wasn't truly decadent and in need of the moral law. Jesus did, however, frequently invite people everywhere to follow Him, to emulate His perfect observance of the commandments through a life of abiding trust in His heavenly Father.

Repose rather than impose. No one held the law of God in higher esteem than did Jesus. He consistently kept the law and taught others to do the same. To those who sought to nullify the Ten Commandments, our Lord underscored their unchanging nature. For those who mistakenly believed that law-keeping was a means of salvation, He described His Messianic mission as laying down His life for the sins of the whole world, including scrupulous law keepers.

To those who had turned the law into a tiresome list of "dos" and "don'ts," Christ said in clear, liberating tones, "Come unto Me and you will find rest for your souls." He taught that the Sabbath of the Decalogue was for celebrating God's salvation, not earning it. His spiritual rest was about reposing by faith in God's grace through His appointed, perfect, paschal Lamb. Never once did

Christ dismiss or diminish the law and not once did He seek to impose it on others. His kingdom, He proclaimed, was one of grace, truth, and the awesome freedom to choose.

Show rather than tell. Jesus didn't print up bumper stickers so His disciples could "share their faith." He wasn't bashful about the law, it's just that the Creator knew best how to win back His wayward creatures. The integrity of His faithful life of obedience to His Father's will made ordinary people want to follow Him. Not a petition drive, not a lapel pin, not a two-ton monument in a public building, and not a national holiday. Jesus "walked the walk"! And His relatively few words on this subject had power and authority precisely because they were consistent with His example. When He encouraged others to thoughtfully observe God's law, He had already shown them how by the way He lived His life.

Shine rather than whine. Our Savior didn't moralistically whine about the moral decline of the world around Him or the evils of a secular government. He didn't join the picket lines, He didn't form a political action committee, and He didn't rally the troops to decry the decay of culture. In fact, He directed His most severe critiques of culture at the ones who should have been most positively influencing culture but who, in attitude and action, appeared to have conformed to the spirit of this world. "Let your light so shine before men, that they may see your good works and glorify your Father in heaven." Influence is a matter of shining more than whining.

Motivate with love rather than law. Better than any of us, Jesus understood that law is a terrible motivator. "If you love Me," Jesus said, you will want to keep My commandments (see John 14:15). Love is the great motivator in our lives and the great transformer of culture. Not law. Not guilt. Not shame. Not rhetoric. Not slogans. Just love!

It is ironic that the zeal of our advocacy for something inherently holy and just and good (Romans 7:12) could easily turn into just another form of legalism and defeat the very purpose for which we strive unless we look to Jesus' example and act as wisely as serpents and as harmless as doves. If we insist that people who claim no connection with Christ must nevertheless observe the Ten Commandments, we end up advocating legalism, a form of godliness without the power of a living relationship with God, wrought by grace through faith in Jesus Christ.

What Would Jesus Do?

A few years ago it was hard to go anywhere without seeing a plethora of lapel pins sporting the letters WWJD, popular shorthand for a serious moral consideration: "What would Jesus do?" This continues to be one of the most important questions sincere followers of Christ can ask.

Later the lapel pin of choice was a golden rendition of Moses' two tablets of stone, indicating the wearer's support for the Ten Commandments. This pin was minted by the hundreds of thousands in preparation for the first annual Ten Commandments Day.

I have already offered some recommendations beyond sloganism, lapel pins, special agendas, or even commemorative events in the previous article "Keeping the Commandments." Now, with particular reference to the fourth commandment and the biblical Lord's Day Sabbath (the only one of the ten that has really divided sincere believers through the ages), please permit a few further thoughts on how to best commemorate the Decalogue.

Written in our hearts rather than on our lawns. The devout group in which our Lord grew up advertised the Ten Commandments constantly. They tied the Decalogue (in miniature, of course) to their foreheads and wrapped it around their wrists for all to see. And then Jesus came.

The Savior advocated a new covenant experience in which God would put His law in the minds of His people and write it on their hearts (Jeremiah 31:33). He promoted more than a lapel pin, more than a monument on the lawn of the county courthouse, more than an annual event. Jesus called His followers to a Spirit-born experience whereby hearts and minds once hostile to God's law could be transformed by grace to the point where the Ten Commandments were embraced, internalized, and lived out in loving service to God and others.

A weekly celebration rather than a yearly festival. God certainly knows how to construct annual, or yearly, festivals. As part of the ceremonial ordinances, He instituted the Passover, the Feast of Tabernacles, and the Day of Atonement, for example. Scripture clearly notes, however, that these annual feasts were in addition to the weekly, seventh-day Sabbath of the Decalogue. "The LORD said to Moses, 'Give the Israelites instructions regarding the LORD's appointed festivals, the days when all of you will be summoned to worship me. You may work for six days each week, but on the seventh day all work must come to a complete stop. It is the LORD's Sabbath day of complete rest, a holy day to assemble for worship. It must be observed wherever you live. In addition to the Sabbath, the LORD has established festivals, the holy occasions to be observed at the proper time each year' " (Leviticus 23:1–4, NLT).

Much confusion would be avoided and multiple blessings would be experienced if this clear distinction were maintained between the weekly Lord's Day Sabbath and these annual feasts that foreshadowed Jesus' sacrifice.

Don't budge, but don't judge. Any believer should worship according to their own convictions without attempting to impose those convictions upon others. While I am personally persuaded that the New Testament did nothing to remove or relocate the weekly Sabbath day (remember Jesus' instructions that His followers should pray that in times of future difficulty they would not have to flee during the extremes of winter or on the Sabbath), nevertheless, I am equally persuaded that my opinion should not control your behavior. Scripture is clear that I may not judge you, nor may you judge me in these matters (Romans 14; Colossians 2).

So, should we observe Ten Commandments Day? Yes! The answer is inherent in the query "What would Jesus do?" Jesus' example (Luke 4:16) and the fourth commandment make it clear—"the seventh day is the Sabbath of the Lord thy God." It is Jesus' day. And Jesus' way!

SECTION III:
REACHING OUT

Lessons From My Bank

Simple mathematics illustrate why we must prioritize children. When we lead an adult to Christ, we add a soul, but when we bring a child to Jesus, we introduce a multiplier for decades to come.

Too often we hear the adage that our children are the church's future. I disagree. I believe that our children are the present church and that we dare not await the future to plan, emphasize, budget, and implement age-appropriate ministry.

Of course, in some areas of the world we invest a great percentage of resources in Christian education; and we recognize this as essential. However, many areas offer no Adventist education below college level, and even where primary education opportunities abound, only a relatively small percentage enrolls.

To reconsider how we approach ministering to and with our children, think like a banker. When I enter my bank, I am inundated with placards and slogans describing the various services the institution provides.

Compound dividends. When the church provides children's ministries, we build for the future. This should not be considered a short-term, shortsighted view.

Savings account. We should view every child as a potential candidate for the kingdom. Perhaps this sounds too simplistic. But remember, Satan targets the very youngest. Surely, we can do our best to save those whom he aims to destroy.

Investment, not expense. Attract youngsters to your church and the adults will follow. Parents want to go where their children want to go. If you plan age-appropriate ministries and activities, parents will vote their support of your leadership with both their feet and their funds!

Mission, not money. My financial institution speaks much more about service to their customers than about holding my money. Of course they want my money, but they emphasize the benefits they provide. If we provide quality benefits for children, the necessary funds will be provided.

Safe depository. We must guarantee the security of precious assets. Volunteers and caregivers must be recruited, screened, and paired with other leaders to ensure that no little one is abused or molested. Training, supervision, and accountability must be hallmarks of all we do for children.

Needs-based service. In our last congregation, my wife, Sharon, an associate pastor of the church, listened to the needs of the parents in our church. She began offering weekly children's worship services plus qualified child care that permitted parents to participate in the worship services. She secured qualified nursery leaders and coordinated those who conducted the weekly children's worship. One bonus came when the nursery attendants asked to become members.

Long-term amortization. Every church has families who need tuition assistance to enable their children's school attendance. Rather than aid grants, we provided age-appropriate work-study for students in grades five through eight. Students could empty trash, clean chalk boards, grade papers, or perform simple tasks to assist teachers. Others volunteered at the church office to fold bulletins, answer phones, or prepare for special events. One mother recently reported that her now adult daughter had become a manager in a government office and credited her church office tasks for providing the first basic skills of interaction, planning, and implementation.

Community involvement. Whatever we do, we should include the whole church community. In our congregation, every service includes youth who provide scripture, music, or even the occasional sermon.

One-stop service. My bank provides a myriad of services at one convenient location. Surely we can demonstrate closer cooperation between school, Sabbath services, Adventurers, children's mission and outreach activities, Pathfinders, Vacation Bible School, and social functions to attract and involve all members of our families.

Start small. A new associate on our staff opened a bank account with just one dollar. All the benefits the bank offered came his way because of that small beginning. You can do the same thing. Do something right now with children's ministry even if you cannot do everything. Begin today and watch your results grow.

Fees and charges. The bank made it clear that there is a cost attached to the benefits they provide. Invest in your church's children. Provide the most attractive rooms and materials. Affirm your teachers and volunteers. Add opportunities beyond the routine events. Spend in order to save.

If you invest in your children, you will reap great dividends. You can count on it!

Over There

One laity leader, having recently returned from a short-term mission venture, wrote to express dismay about circumstances over there that were very different from his expectations. He also noted that church headquarters should immediately fix the injustices that he had observed.

I replied both to thank him for his eagerness to serve and to note that some good things had resulted despite some challenges. On the other hand, I grieved that advance information left guests unprepared to face the realities they encountered in areas where funds are in very short supply to accommodate those who arrive from other cultures or economic realities. I also explained that leaders at headquarters cannot resolve issues in which independent ministries, not the church structure, control the entire process.

For example, my correspondent mentioned great numbers of students with multichurch responsibilities who receive little or no pay. While this is a tragedy, both their dedication and the reality that dozens of other would-be ministers are prepared to step into their place means these young pastors are willing to work for little pay. With no other jobs available in their economy, they have matriculated through their training with hope that eventually they will become fully employed.

Of course this is not equitable, but this reality says that if these young pastors were to quit working for an irregular bit of income, likely they would have no income from any employment. This system cannot be described as either appropriate or workable for the long term, but describes a reality for many entry-level ministers in various parts of the world. If they quit, others will quickly jump at the opportunity to replace them.

The writer also complained that only US$1,000 was allocated for the project, and that amount certainly failed to cover the needs. He demanded to know why the church permitted such poor planning. Of course, these challenges must be addressed by the independent groups who organize such ventures rather than expecting the denomination to monitor the policies and procedures of entities that it does not control nor govern their utilization of funds. While much good is accomplished by such projects, numerous problems arise from situations in which the hosts are expected to cover deficits that they are incapable of funding.

My correspondent also expressed concern about local expectations that guests pay various expenses such as food, tourist entry fees, incidental expenses, etc. This seemed strange to him, for in his culture, hosts provide for their guests. However, the local people have no resources with which to host those who appear to have such abundance.

I feel certain that these hosts are not unwilling to pay for their guests, but simply do not have the funds. On a day-to-day basis, their hosts would never eat in a restaurant, visit a tourist site, or purchase souvenirs. They simply would have no money for such functions, so when foreigners arrive and desire locals to accompany them as translators or guides, the guests must provide for all costs for both the group as well as their hosts. I wish each tour group could understand this reality in advance so they are not disappointed once they arrive over there.

Each group should receive advance instructions regarding expectations as well and plan on financing every anticipated need plus unforeseen circumstances. Limited local funds must not be taxed, but rather covered by the guests. This includes stipends for student pastors, extra expenses for local leaders, transportation for those attending evangelistic programs, auditorium rental, supplies, books and Bibles, and most important, adequate church homes for new believers to assemble once the guests depart. (I recently led a group of guests who completed their short venture with a long-term commitment to build/purchase a house of worship.)

Perhaps the greatest strength of short mission trips lies in the large numbers of members who travel and gain a firsthand insight into the Lord's work and come home with a new vision for mission. Perhaps the greatest weakness is the concept that a short-term commitment of a few weeks is all that is necessary for the church over there.

In reality, these programs should be viewed in terms of years and include thorough preparation and orientation as well as ongoing efforts to purchase or build suitable places of worship and establish every new believer in the faith. We need far fewer projects, in my opinion, and then we should couple these with far longer implementation and follow-through to make full reality of our endeavors to build disciples for Christ and His kingdom.

The Numbers Game

Peter Wagner describes an encounter with an individual who declared his disgust against numbers: "My Bible tells me to feed the sheep, not to count them!"

Later, Wagner read Philip Keller's book *A Shepherd Looks at Psalm 23*. Keller, a professional sheep rancher, says it is "essential for a careful shepherd to look over his flock every day, counting them to see that all are able to be up and on their feet." Wagner points out, "I believe that counting sheep is such a natural part of the shepherd's life that Jesus took for granted His followers would know that. It is biblical to feed the sheep, but also to count them."[1]

In fact, the only way that the Good Shepherd knew that He had one lost sheep was because He had counted the other ninety-nine. "God Himself does a lot of counting. He even has the hairs on each person's head numbered. When each individual comes to faith in Jesus Christ, that name is written in the Lamb's book of life. Even the littlest person is important in heaven and gets individual recognition. There is joy in heaven over one sinner who repents (Luke 15:7), so somebody there must be keeping close track. As I see it, those who object to numbers are usually trying to avoid superficiality in Christian commitment. . . . I am vitally interested in lost men and women who put their faith in Jesus Christ and are born again. I am interested in true disciples who take up their cross daily to follow Jesus. I am interested in kingdom people who relate to Jesus as their Lord. I am interested in Spirit-filled people who have experienced the power of the Holy Spirit and are using their spiritual gifts. I am interested in responsible church members who continue 'steadfastly in the apostles' doctrine and fellowship, in breaking of bread, and in prayers' (Acts 2:42) as did believers in the Jerusalem church. When numbers represent these kinds of people, they are much more than a 'numbers game.' They become a game of life and death, a game of time or eternity."[2]

When Jesus commanded His disciples to go into all the world and make disciples of all nations, He was concerned about numbers—numbers of persons who would become disciples. To those who criticize, Bailey Smith has given an appropriate response: "Let's never forget that numbers are all multi-

---

1. C. Peter Wagner, *Leading Your Church to Growth* (Ventura, Calif.: Regal Books, 1984), 22, 23.
2. Ibid., 23, 24.

ples of one. One hundred is a hundred ones; a thousand, a thousand ones; so it is possible to be honestly concerned about each one of several thousand ones. We need concern for all!"[3]

In the Great Commission Christ clearly mandates that His church should multiply, not simply maintain. The book of Acts is the story of rapid church growth—and it talks about numbers! "About three thousand were added to their number that day" (Acts 2:41, NIV). "The Lord added to their number daily" (verse 47, NIV). "Many . . . believed, and the number of men grew to about five thousand" (4:4, NIV). "More and more men and women believed in the Lord and were added to their number" (5:14, NIV). "The number of disciples . . . increased rapidly, and a large number of priests became obedient to the faith" (6:7, NIV). "The church . . . grew in numbers, living in the fear of the Lord" (9:31). "A great number of people believed" (11:21). "So the churches . . . grew daily in numbers" (16:5). The message is obvious. If the church is going to be interested in what interests Jesus, it will be interested in numbers—numbers of people for His kingdom!

Tom Stebbins says, "Someone has suggested that before we can win people to Jesus Christ we must win them to ourselves. Sharing the gospel is a very personal matter. We are probing the most intimate, private areas of the other person's life so we must first earn that person's trust and build some measure of friendship."[4]

Therefore, our evangelistic methods must transform unbelievers into friends, friends into believers, and believers into disciples—great numbers of disciples! If we embrace only one primary evangelistic strategy—prophetic-based gospel proclamation and doctrinal instruction—we face two dangers: we risk limiting those whom we could win and we risk losing those whom we have already won!

Friendship involvement may become our most effective strategy for evangelizing new believers, and group interaction is a proven method for making disciples. The principle remains. New members must have something more than head knowledge regarding what they believe. Meaningful relationships and ministry tasks are not only the fruit of a disciplined individual but also the methodology for accomplishing that discipleship. These relationships and tasks are the process! This process is the product!

3. Bailey E. Smith, *Real Evangelism* (Nashville, Tenn.: Broadman, 1978), 121.

4. Tom Stebbins, *Evangelism by the Book* (Camp Hill, Pa.: Christian Publications, 1991), 218.

Evangelizing Preparation

When I heard John Sweigart use the term *Evangeliving,* I knew it conveys the best definition for teaching evangelism as process more than event.

During our years as itinerate evangelists, Sharon and I often grieved at the suppositions that we could deliver one event to encompass the totality of evangelistic endeavor. Leaders and members embraced this assumption: paying and praying for our success. Typically, however, neither group addressed the holistic necessity of evangelism as a thoroughly integrated process of sowing, reaping, and conserving.

And frankly, itinerating guests who shorten public preaching to an even briefer "touch and go" event only perpetuate the assumption that high-quality proclamation—conveying truth in the most attractive, winsome package possible—is all that is needed for evangelistic success. A possible theme song for such an approach could be "Information Saves!"

Vampire Christianity. Of course, such has never been our theological position, but this "event mentality" has clearly infected our practice. Anthony B. Robinson cites Dallas Willard's new book, *The Great Omission,* which describes a prevalent gospel reductionism focusing primarily on conversion and eternal salvation while neglecting belief as a way of life here and now.

Willard terms this shortsighted focus on conversion at the neglect of thoroughgoing discipleship as "vampire Christianity" in which the individual says to Jesus, in effect, "I'd like a little of your blood, but I don't care to be your student . . . in fact, won't you just excuse me while I get on with my life, and I'll see you in heaven."[1]

So I cheered when the North American Division of the Seventh-day Adventist Church voted for a three-year comprehensive process of preparation, proclamation, and preservation while emphasizing the concurrent necessity of all three in continuous cycle.

Great goals, poor slogan. Unfortunately, the terminology designating the Year of Pastoral Evangelism may dissuade more than persuade. Some ministers may react and assume the proposal imposes more work on an already overextended pastoral force while conveying the idea that laity may relax, fund, and observe or ignore the efforts of professional pastors.

Designating pastoral evangelism perpetuates the myth that ministers can

---

1. Anthony B. Robinson, "Follow Me," *The Christian Century,* September 4, 2007, 23.

accomplish the objectives alone. Regardless of the worthy objectives, such terminology implies limitations on releasing all believers into the fields. Jesus instructs us to pray for more reapers, not to impose descriptive confines as to who is responsible. Here's reality! If we wait for pastors alone to do the work, we will wait in our graves.

Of course, ministers have a leadership function—nothing happened at the crossing of the Jordan until the priests' feet entered the water. But the people were delivered only when they followed in eager participation. Therefore, I encourage the encompassing vision of all believers becoming engaged in evangeliving.

Preparation needed. Regardless of the need for better sloganeering, we can embrace the concept as beneficial. As ministers, we have a wonderful opportunity to intentionally prepare for a truly abundant harvest. While encouraging this integrated process, the following specifics will prepare us for an outpouring of evangeliving blessings:

Repentance. Let us acknowledge our sin and seek the face of our Savior in repentance for our willingness to maintain the status quo or to excuse small results. Let us seek forgiveness and expect victorious living.

Review. Let us remember and rehearse the abundant blessings of the Lord's leading in our past and acknowledge our dependence upon His favor for our future.

Revival. Let us preach Jesus alone as the Source of all the church needs to accomplish God's plan for seeking the lost, and let us never stray from a Christ-centered focus.

Reformation. Let us call our members to live our lives congruent with our convictions and let us lead by example, fasting from those things that detract from Jesus or that deny the Spirit's transforming power.

Relationship. Let us restore everyday evangeliving. Make acquaintance with strangers until they become our friends. Invite friends to attend until they are included in church life, even before they become believers.

Renewal. Let us do things differently and expect different results. Plan annual events in which to preach good news. Conduct intense Weeks of Spiritual Emphasis and Prayer. Teach how to emulate Jesus.

Revamp. Let us rearrange priorities until committees become strategizing sessions for mission rather than boards to grant or withhold permission about lesser issues.

Reliance. Let us seek God's will and God's way, asking the Holy Spirit to help us view people through Heaven's eyes, considering every contact a candidate for the kingdom. If you are concerned about funds, concentrate on the potential—the money we need to accomplish God's will is already in the mouths of the fish we are called to catch.

Reap. Let us determine that evangeliving will define our lives and drive our preaching. Call for decisions. Concentrate on the cities—going where the people are. Expect sizeable results.

Rejoice. Let us expect great things from God and boldly venture forward to rejoice in all He will provide.

Instruction That Prepares and Preserves

If the instruction of new believers produces isolationism or feelings of superiority, it has failed in its objective. Although knowing the truth will set you free, none can ever be saved only by the information they possess.

Nevertheless, instruction is necessary. In fact, it is vital and foundational. Jesus' commission commands His followers to make disciples, to baptize, and to teach all things that He has commanded (Matthew 28:19, 20). The obvious question is when and where that teaching occurs.

Ellen White stated, "After the first efforts have been made in a place by giving a course of lectures, there is really greater necessity for a second course than for the first. The truth is new and startling, and the people need to have the same presented the second time, to get the points distinct and the ideas fixed in the mind."[1]

Michael Green's research points out that in the early days of Christianity, baptism was administered straight away on profession of faith and repentance and that this practice continued at least throughout the first century. "However, the Didache suggests that very soon a period of instruction in the Christian faith, particularly its ethical side, preceded baptism. It would not be surprising if the early missionaries did soon evolve a stylized form of Christian instruction just as they seem to have done, at least to some extent, with their gospel preaching."[2]

Green's additional comment on this indoctrination process of the early church comes directly to the crux of the issue for Adventists. He says, "Whether it [this indoctrination instruction] preceded baptism or followed it is more problematical."[3]

Adventist evangelism has followed a similar process of providing baptismal preparation instruction simultaneously with gospel proclamation. For example, a new member in my congregation once observed, "Your evangelistic series is, in reality, an inquirer's class."

In fact, the very issue of how much of that instruction should precede baptism and how much should be provided as the newly baptized believer grows has been a vigorously debated topic among Adventists for more than a generation. Sometimes we have invested more energy in the debate than we have in the actual process of grounding new believers.

---

1. Ellen G. White, *Evangelism* (Washington, D.C.: Review and Herald®, 1970), 334.
2. Michael Green, *Evangelism in the Early Church* (Grand Rapids, Mich.: Eerdmans, 1970), 154.
3. Ibid.

Long-term church members essentially want all instruction to precede baptism. But this has brought problems to the process of assimilating new members. The greatest of these problems may be the inability of the new believer to grasp everything in a relatively short period of indoctrination. Consider the necessity of repetition as a learning process for infants.

However, the most dangerous of these problems may well be the erroneous conclusion that since converts are so thoroughly indoctrinated prior to baptism, they need no additional or further post-baptismal instruction or that we might consider it safe to leave new believers on their own. Of course, the more we shorten the pre-baptism proclamation phase, the more essential becomes the post-baptism indoctrination and assimilation phase.

Our responsibility is dual: we must proclaim the truth, and we must assimilate the new believers into the culture—the culture of the church versus the world, the culture of discipleship versus nominalism, the culture of the experience and expression of faith within the fellowship of the local congregation as well as within the wider body of all Christians.

The content of instruction is important as well. It should be geared both to the level of comprehension and to the level of commitment of the new believer.

Further, there should be a core understanding and consensus by the body as to what is essential and what is additional. Herb Miller says, "Trying to get people to 'have the mind of Christ' on moral matters is admirable. But we must always be wary that we are not really trying to get them to 'have our mind' on the matter instead of His. Many who think they are witnessing to God's word are really trying to speak God's word for Him. That subtle form of idol worship tries to take over God's job of being God. 'Accept among you the man who is weak in the faith, but do not argue with him about his personal opinions' (Rom. 14:1) is still excellent advice. Pride in our own righteousness has no place in word communication."[4]

However, Jesus' own words (Matthew 28:19, 20) anticipate an instruction that comes after baptism as well as that necessary to baptize the convert. The words "teaching them to observe all things" (KJV) do not precede the experience of baptism in the gospel commission and, for all practical purposes, cannot precede new birth in the actual life of the believer.

To me, this becomes theologically persuasive with a definite practical application. If baptism brings a spiritual rebirth (John 3), and if spiritual things are spiritually discerned (1 Corinthians 2:14), then some portion of the "all things" that Jesus has commanded cannot be discerned until the individual experiences that *spiritual rebirth.*

To attempt to do otherwise ignores the process envisioned by the gospel commission.

---

4. Herb Miller, *Evangelism's Open Secrets* (St. Louis, Mo.: CBP Press, 1977), 40. Bible text from CEV.

How to Guarantee a Crowd

A small framed illustration hanging in my office depicts delivery men unloading mannequins from a delivery van. The lettering on the van says "Rent a Crowd."

As congregations prepare to conduct public evangelistic meetings, we need better methods for bringing people into our venues. I have found the following methods help guarantee an audience:

Pray. Nothing is more successful in arresting the attention of potential converts than enlisting the power of God upon your venture. Form your church's prayer warriors into groups and set them loose to support every aspect of evangelism with earnest prayer for the Holy Spirit's outpouring.

Relevant topics. We live in prophetically momentous times. Don't be content to rehash old sermons or repeat illustrations from the past. Even the mighty evangelistic heroes of bygone eras will not sound as fresh as the topics you develop to address current issues. Read your newspaper along with your Bible and make the messages you preach significant for today.

Share your personal experience. Sharon and I discovered that we can significantly increase attendance by advertising an upcoming sermon in which we share our personal story. To those who attend your series, you become a personality in whom they are interested. We show our baby pictures, photos of our wedding, our pets, our ministry adventures, and tell the story of God's leading in our personal lives. Then, after a dozen or so slides about us, we transition into the call of God into ministry and the amazing gift of His grace for our lives, which easily introduces the concept of personal salvation.

Offer a valuable service. Whether a simple blood pressure check and glaucoma screening or a more complex battery of health options, a practical service provided as a component of public proclamation demonstrates interest in the welfare of your attendees and makes a fine introduction to a regular "healthful living" feature.

Valuable gift. Avoid prize drawings or lotteries, but do encourage attendance by providing everyone a gift of spiritual value if they are present for a compelling sermon series. I always present the Lord's Day as a two-part sermon and provide each attendee with a complimentary copy of *Your Bible & You* or *Bible Readings for the Home.* Such books may seem ordinary to you but are compelling to those seeking truth. Remember, the content of the gift is more important than the monetary value. Again, when I present the spiritual gift of prophetic guidance, I give each attendee a copy of *Steps to Christ.*

Film series. I've discovered the power of a continuing series, such as the film *JESUS,* especially in areas of the world where the basic gospel story may be unknown. People will arrive early to witness these compelling scenes from our Savior's ministry.

Arresting titles. The purpose of titles is to catch the attention of potential attendees. Sermon titles may range from the ridiculous to the sublime depending on the culture in which you preach. I once heard a very successful preacher advertise his topic on man's condition in death as "Is There Sex After Death?" Attendance grew mightily when he approached a basic Bible message with such verve. Personally, I prefer "Real Hope for Your Lonely Life: If You Have Ever Lost a Loved One, Here's Hope for You."

Visuals. Your preaching will make a greater impact if you utilize visuals to convey the message. Adventists have historically used prophecy charts and other visuals to illustrate great Bible themes. Fresh, innovative illustrations allow you to cover more information because your audience sees the texts on screen as they hear you preach.

Cash. Have you ever been paid to attend church? When I approach the topic of stewardship, I announce in advance, "I intend to talk about money, but not your money. And to illustrate this concept, I will pay you my own money to hear this sermon." Then, I give each attendee a ten-cent coin that quickly and disarmingly demonstrates the relatively small 10 percent tithe that God asks us to return in comparison to the abundant blessings He guarantees for faithfulness. This light-hearted, chuckle-producing illustration disarms as it instructs.

Bible marking. We give each individual a personal Bible and open each topic with a class highlighting essential texts on the sermon theme. As everyone underlines and make notes in the margin, Scripture comes alive.

Open agendas. Announce your intentions clearly and avoid disguising your identity or purpose. How much better to clearly advertise that you are inviting the public to explore Bible truths? Personally, I've found that conducting my evangelistic activities in Adventist facilities reassures the public that an established church is sponsoring this special event.

Biblical authority. Base each presentation firmly on God's Word. Shun sermons that wander into speculation. Build confidence by referencing the Bible, comparing Scripture with Scripture, and by affirming the Holy Spirit's power to awaken our hearts to understand what Jesus wants us to experience.

Take-home lessons. During the first week of our series, we provide each person a Bible study guide to complete at home and bring back when they return to the meetings. I challenge participants to complete the lessons as a method for learning to study the Bible for themselves. The lessons emphasize the messages presented and enable the Holy Spirit to speak to each individual as they study.

Preach benefits. More than by merely reciting facts, people are warmed and won by proclaiming the benefits behind factual features. For example, hope beyond death's grief brings joy when I explain how Jesus regards the benefit of reunion for myself and my loved ones as so important that He personally guarantees the resurrection—the Lord, Himself, descends from heaven to raise the righteous and catches the living up together with them.

Experimentation. When presenting messages that compel behavioral change, share the process as well as the expectation. As I invite people to consider keeping the seventh-day Sabbath, I encourage them to experience the Lord's Day for themselves by providing opportunities to enjoy a Sabbath blessing. Rather than asking for a commitment to a reality they have not yet experienced, I encourage tasting and seeing that the Lord is good.

Fellowship. While people learn much through proclamation, they absorb more through interaction and discussion. After-meeting times of conversation, light refreshments, questions, and fellowship accomplish much in settling the message into the minds and attitudes of attendees. Such opportunities awaken conviction.

Goals. Encourage faith-stretching objectives. We ask members to pray specifically for those they will invite and to reach out actively and winsomely to their family, friends, and associates expecting heaven to honor their endeavors with fruit for the kingdom. Attempt great things for God. Expect great things from God.

Culturally relevant incentives. In some locales, we have encouraged the most popular person in the city to invite all of his or her friends. Then, we recognize the person with the most guests as "Mr./Ms. Congeniality" and give them a special gift for having demonstrated their influence.

Unique experiences. A fellowship banquet featuring healthful recipes makes an inviting introduction to Adventist lifestyle. We always include a Communion service as part of the evangelistic series with advance notice that Adventists celebrate open Communion and we invite any believer to participate.

Family orientation. Our colleagues, Ron and Karen Flowers, prepared a helpful book, *Family Evangelism,*[1] which presents techniques of using family systems rather than individuality as an evangelistic tool. While the Western world seems to glory in the individual acting alone upon their convictions, the New Testament presents another approach of leaders bringing their whole

---

1. Ron and Karen Flowers, *Family Evangelism* (Silver Spring, Md.: Department of Family Ministries of the General Conference of Seventh-day Adventists, 2003).

extended family with them into discipleship. Providing infant care and attractive children's programming signals parents that you desire to benefit their entire family.

Attractive advertising. Your promotional strategies dictate the crowds you attract. Sensationalized portrayals of lurid scenes may detract those who would be open to another emphasis. For example, instead of depicting fierce beasts, our evangelistic brochure features a dad embracing his wife and kids with their puppy. Attendees arrive expecting practical benefits.

Practical topics. Emphasize Bible answers for real-life situations. Discover the powerful impact of topics that provide scriptural methods for successful living—how to face the future with greater confidence; how to have your prayers answered; how your family can be secure. Such titles attract those who are looking for answers.

Enlist support. When an Adventist hospital, school, or publishing institution exists in the community, I always feature these leaders, and they invite their contacts. I also contact spiritual television and radio programs to request a special letter of invitation to their lists. I even ask my fellow pastors of other denominations to notify their congregations that I am beginning a special series in my church designed for the entire community.

Sequence of presentations. Begin with practical and prophetic topics that build confidence in Bible authority and are common to most believers such as the assurance of God's love and providence in Daniel 2 or the hope and signs of Jesus coming in Matthew 24. Next, preach distinctive truths that anticipate convicting choices and conclude your series with deeply spiritual decision sermons that motivate a determination to follow Jesus.

Christ-centered. Keep Jesus the central focus of every sermon. Make His power and the joy of walking with Him as your Savior and Lord the theme and appeal of every message. You will discover real power and amazing results from lifting up Jesus.

Power-filled Church Growth

In preparing for evangelism, remember that personal work is as essential as public proclamation.

Society's situation does not demand an either/or approach. We need effective preaching to the masses, and we need effective personal ministry to individuals.

By reliance upon God's power, our efforts become His work from initiation to completion. "There is need of coming close to the people by personal effort. If less time were given to sermonizing, and more time were spent in personal ministry, greater results would be seen. The poor are to be relieved, the sick cared for, the sorrowing and the bereaved comforted, the ignorant instructed, the inexperienced counseled. We are to weep with those that weep, and rejoice with those that rejoice. Accompanied by the power of persuasion, the power of prayer, the power of the love of God, this work will not, cannot, be without fruit."[1]

God provides the power. "But you shall receive power when the Holy Spirit has come upon you" (Acts 1:8, NKJV). With the Holy Spirit we can accomplish everything; without Him we can accomplish nothing.

God provides the process. "And you shall be witnesses to Me in Jerusalem, and in all Judea and Samaria, and to the end of the earth" (verse 8, NKJV). Begin at home. Follow the natural sequence of first reaching your own family, friends, neighbors, and colleagues. Then expand wider until, ultimately, the entire world is lightened by the gospel.

God provides the promise. "This same Jesus, who was taken up from you into heaven, will so come in like manner as you saw Him go into heaven" (verse 11, NKJV). Jesus' own promise to gloriously culminate His kingdom at His second coming motivates our ministry.

God provides the premise. "These all continued with one accord in prayer and supplication, with the women and Mary the mother of Jesus, and with His brothers" (verse 14, NKJV). Start where His first followers started—with unity, prayer, and seeking the Holy Spirit.

God provides the proclamation. "Then Peter said unto them, 'Repent, and let every one of you be baptized in the name of Jesus Christ for the remission of sins' " (2:38, NKJV). The content of our preaching is specific and clear: Jesus, repentance, and baptism!

God provides the prophecy. "And you shall receive the gift of the Holy Spirit.

---

1. Ellen G. White, *The Ministry of Healing* (Nampa, Idaho: Pacific Press®, 1942), 143, 144.

For the promise is to you and to your children" (verses 38, 39, NKJV). The same gifts that the Holy Spirit poured out upon Christ's church at its inception are available to Christ's church today.

God provides the projection. "And to all who are afar off, as many as the Lord our God will call" (verse 39, NKJV). Scripture envisions a saving message that encircles and enlightens the entire globe.

God provides the purpose. "He testified and exhorted them, saying, 'Be saved from this perverse generation' "(verse 40, NKJV). Devise bold initiatives that are for the specific purpose of saving people.

God provides the persuasion. "Then those who gladly received his word were baptized" (verse 41, NKJV). At Pentecost, Peter's preaching was so powerful that his listeners happily acted upon their convictions.

God provides the product. "And that day about three thousand souls were added to them" (verse 41, NKJV). Abundant results follow relying upon God's plan.

God provides the program. "And they continued steadfastly in the apostles' doctrine and fellowship, in the breaking of bread, and in prayers" (verse 42, NKJV). Organized, determined efforts to disciple new believers include: Bible study—preaching and teaching. Prayer—seeking the Holy Spirit. Fellowship—visitation and nurture. Witnessing—telling of God's blessings. Obedience—developing believers into disciples.

God provides the proof. "Then fear came upon every soul, and many wonders and signs were done through the apostles" (verse 43, NKJV). Marvelous manifestations accompany life-changing experiences.

God provides the portion. "Now all who believed were together, and had all things in common" (verse 44, NKJV). A unified church sees to the needs of all.

God provides the participation. "And sold their possessions and goods, and divided them among all, as anyone had need" (verse 45, NKJV). A unified church encourages all to share and to sacrifice.

God provides the presence. "So continuing daily with one accord in the temple, and breaking bread from house to house, they ate their food with gladness and simplicity of heart" (verse 46, NKJV). Jesus remains in the midst of His people through the indwelling of His Spirit.

God provides the praise. "Praising God and having favor with all the people" (verse 47, NKJV). Living in praise brings joy in our journey and favor among all who observe.

God provides the prosperity. "And the Lord added to the church daily those who were being saved" (verse 47, NKJV). Heaven envisions an ongoing process, more than a one-time event.

God provides Himself as the prize. "Behold, the tabernacle of God is with men, and He will dwell with them, and they shall be His people. God Himself will be with them and be their God" (Revelation 21:3, NKJV).

How Do You Spell Relief?

When four Florida hurricanes destroyed his crop, Dale Bass, owner of Golden Harvest Fruit Company, realized he was "out of business" until the next season. As the premier shipper of high-quality citrus to churches and schools for fund-raising, Dale also understood that many entities would feel the impact as they, in turn, suffered from the lack of shipments and the short-fall of needed income.

Even with no fruit to ship, the business must maintain its contacts, care for its employees, and assure future deliveries. More immediate in the disaster, however, was the trauma of lost homes, jobs, transportation, heirlooms, communication, pets, and even lives. Charitable and governmental agencies move into such disaster areas to provide rescue and long-term rebuilding aid; but even before they arrive, congregations can provide specific help if pre-crisis planning has occurred.

"How do you spell relief?" This very slogan of the famous antacid medicine recognizes that the first great need may be to reduce pressure.

In the midst of disaster, many people become disoriented, experiencing both emotional and physical shock. Victims do not always respond with logic to devastating events. For example, in these same hurricanes, Sharon's seventy-something-year-old mother decided she would climb onto her house roof to check the damage caused by a falling tree. While insurance agencies would clearly warn church volunteers against becoming roof-repairers, I would much rather a younger neighbor had climbed that ladder than a senior citizen.

Where do you start? Dale says, "When someone has lost everything, that is exactly what they need—every thing! A bottle of water, a thermos of soup, a place to sleep." His Fort Pierce congregation opened its facilities for people to sleep on the pews, established a hot-meal program in the neighborhoods, and began to serve rescuers who had come to work the larger effort. There's a whole lot of religion in a loaf of bread. Add peanut butter and jelly and they will never forget you.

Sometimes the greatest kindness is simply "being there" to sit alongside someone who has experienced great loss. Eloquence is not needed. Your very presence communicates care, concern, camaraderie, and confidence in God's providences. As Saint Francis admonished, "Preach the gospel always; if necessary use words." If you must speak, talk of a hope-filled future; of better days to come. Don't preach, but do articulate hope, assurance, and your personal belief in the ultimate triumph of good over tragedy and evil. And do listen. Allow those whose lives have been uprooted to share their pain. Just the ability to talk about their feelings of loss brings them real stress relief.

How do you spell re-live? Simple actions make a great contribution. Try helping sort the debris of a destroyed house for photos, hauling away trash, running errands, providing emergency child care, sharing transportation, loaning your mobile phone, contacting animal shelters, or phoning relatives. By helping victims focus on the future, you enable them to struggle out of the immediate chaos toward restoration of normal life patterns. Clothing, food staples, household supplies, bedding, and kitchen equipment may top the list of needed items. When people begin rebuilding their lives, they need everything.

By advance thinking and planning, your church can organize processes to collect and distribute supplies and money in cooperation with other help agencies. A well-maintained database of care groups, crisis counselors, medical centers, insurance companies, and other volunteer organizations will provide vital information for a future crisis. You can also follow up by offering grief-and-loss-recovery support groups.

How do you spell re-leaf? Dale's citrus groves will re-leaf and produce new fruit. Generous souls will grow again into abundant harvests.

Likewise, a certain "re-leafing" will flourish in your own heart. If you have ministered to strangers through traumatic times, you will discover a host of new friends in whose lives you have invested and in whose souls you have become family. Your own perspective will change concerning life's real essentials as less important issues are eclipsed by the things that really count in life. Opportunities will expand for your congregation to share expertise and to experience fellowship with individuals who, previously, had not been open to the gospel.

And as you plan, remember, "Christ's method alone will give true success in reaching the people. The Saviour mingled with men as one who desired their good. He showed His sympathy for them, ministered to their needs, and won their confidence. Then He bade them, 'Follow Me.' "[1]

---

1. Ellen G. White, *The Ministry of Healing* (Nampa, Idaho: Pacific Press®, 1905), 143.

Smile-Winning

During our first years of ministry, my wife, Sharon, and I were invited to associate on a short-term assignment with a veteran evangelist who would teach us the finer points of obtaining spiritual decisions. We eagerly planned for the six weeks during which we expected to learn new skills and insights into the art of working with people.

Within a few days of joining his team, we quickly came to the realization that we might learn more by observing what *not* to do than by seeking a pattern to emulate. For example, in his public preaching, he would divide his attendees over inconsequential issues such as telling females who were wearing pantsuits that they were bound for perdition and not to return to his meetings if they could not dress appropriately. As you can imagine, the next night about half as many guests attended as the evening before.

Then there was his technique of intimidating decisions from the students at the parochial school where we had been invited to conduct a Week of Prayer. Although I had been given the assignment to present the messages, my supervisor—quite certain I was failing to sufficiently warn the youngsters of the dangers of rejecting his plan to baptize them in the next two weeks—took the platform one morning to announce in the sternest tones imaginable that he had one simple question to ask the kids: "Do you want to go to hell or don't you?"

The students were stunned at an interrogation so incongruent with the messages they had been hearing. Their parents were angry. The teachers asked us not to return. The evangelist decried the Laodicean attitude of all involved. Sharon and I began one-on-one visits with the families in their homes and accomplished more in gaining favorable choices through friendly visitation than could have ever been extracted by hellfire admonition.

I learned that heaven cannot be proclaimed as merely a "fire escape" and that the best motivation for following Jesus springs from a loving, concerned relationship far more than it does from fear or intimidation.

Today, I believe we still have the opportunity to best represent Jesus' character by a joyful countenance and friendly demeanor rather than stern, joyless approaches. I have learned not to argue theology or debate finely divided issues. While I could typically win the argument, I could easily lose a friend in the process.

Jesus' methodology is far different. Instead, He asks us to invite people to share the benefits of knowing our Savior by demonstrating His love and interest in their welfare. "Christ's method alone will give true success in reaching the people. The Saviour mingled with men as one who desired their good. He showed His sympathy for them, ministered to their needs, and won their confidence. Then He bade them, 'Follow Me.' "[1]

Evangelism is a process, and that process begins with making people glad they know me as Christ's ambassador. If they don't like me, they will probably not warm to the idea of knowing my God. Several passages of inspired counsel will help us comprehend the necessity of doing Jesus' work in Jesus' way:

A cultivated intellect is a great treasure; but without the softening influence of sympathy and sanctified love it is not of the highest value. We should have words and deeds of tender consideration for others. We can manifest a thousand little attentions in friendly words and pleasant looks, which will be reflected upon us again. Thoughtless Christians manifest by their neglect of others that they are not in union with Christ. It is impossible to be in union with Christ and yet be unkind to others and forgetful of their rights. Many long intensely for friendly sympathy.[2]

He who is successful in His work for God must be courteous. Courtesy gains access to hearts. The worker for Christ must be to principle as firm as a rock, but at the same time he is to reveal the Saviour's gentleness. He is to be kind as well as true. He is to observe the weightier matters of the law, and he is also to observe the little proprieties of life. Christ desires our lives to be fragrant and refreshing, a blessing to others. The Christian is to be true and honest, and yet kind and forbearing, pitiful and courteous.[3]

We are taught in the Word of God to be kind, tender, pitiful, courteous. Cultivate Christ like love. Let all that you do bear the impress of this love. Those who do not speak the words and do the works of Christ are trying to climb into heaven by some other way than through the door.[4]

---

1. Ellen G. White, *The Ministry of Healing* (Mountain View, Calif.: Pacific Press®, 1942), 143.

2. White, *Mind, Character, and Personality,* vol. 1 (Nashville, Tenn.: Southern Publishing Association, 1977), 85.

3. White, *Manuscript Releases,* vol. 18 (Silver Spring, Md.: Ellen G. White Estate, 1990), 146.

4. White, *This Day With God* (Washington, D.C.: Review and Herald®, 1979), 266.

The religion of Jesus softens whatever is hard and rough in the temper, and smoothes whatever is rugged and sharp in the manners. It makes the words gentle and the demeanor winning. Let us learn from Christ how to combine a high sense of purity and integrity with sunniness of disposition. A kind, courteous Christian is the most powerful argument that can be produced in favor of Christianity.[5]

---

5. White, *Gospel Workers* (Battle Creek, Mich.: Review and Herald®, 1901), 122.

Reconnect, Reclaim, Reflame

While we engage in new evangelist endeavors, we must confront the reality that many who once worshiped with us, now, for a variety of reasons, no longer fellowship with our church, or any other denomination. While we emphasize reaching the lost—sometimes termed our "unsaved loved ones"—we ought to remember the needs of former, missing, or inactive members—our "unloved saved ones"!

Of course, free choice mandates that each individual's right not to worship must be respected, but many of these individuals do not participate in worship or other church activities because they have been hurt, disappointed, or disillusioned at some point along the way. In many cases, we have been the cause of fellow believers leaving active fellowship by our coldness or indifference to their needs.

Why they leave. While doctrinal differences, heretical breakaway groups, or disagreements over worship styles and standards have caused some people to leave, others depart due to boredom, poor preaching, and inadequately planned services. However, the vast majority leave due simply to a lack of friendship. They have been wounded in the church. Whatever the cause for their absence, two things are certain. The back door still swings and solutions lie far more within our power as active members than we might wish to think.

In North America alone, nearly 300,000 members officially have been removed (and not because of death) from our membership in the past twenty years. That total equals 40 percent of our total membership at the beginning of these two decades—a tragedy of greatest proportions, especially when we have not maintained even basic information like a mail or telephone contact. This equals a total loss similar to that of the ten largest conferences in the division simply disappearing.

These numbers, tragic as they are, reveal only part of the story. Also, thousands of individuals are still on the membership rolls who never worship with other believers—only about 50 percent of all members actually attend weekly worship services. Granted, many are ill, elderly, or traveling. This still leaves a vast potential audience of individuals whom God loves and for whom His church ought to feel passion to love back into fellowship.

The great evangelist Fordyce Detamore used to emphasize the *reachability* of former members as his "best potentials" for bringing them to a new relationship with Jesus. So if we want to add 100,000 active members to our churches during this year, we might well start by reaching our "unloved saved ones" with renewed hope in the soon return of Jesus.

While we recognize that some who have left our fellowship would choose not to return, many have left because of interpersonal difficulties—loneliness, alienation, boredom, lack of spiritual food, criticism, rejection, etc. Thousands are waiting on the verge of the kingdom to be invited back. Among these, we can make a difference as we allow the Spirit to work in our lives. We can, and must, actively search for them, listen to them, and hopefully reclaim them into a vital relationship with Christ and His church.

You know who we need! One of the first steps in reclaiming those who were once part of our fellowship is to identify their names and mailing addresses so we can contact them. Your help is needed! Your congregants know the very ones we need. While we have the names and addresses of some of those who should be contacted, many names and addresses are unknown to the church office, even though they are individuals whom your members know personally. Never assume that the church has accurate or up-to-date information. If you know someone who should receive a gracious contact along with a no-pressure invitation to resume fellowship, please let us know.

In our last pastorate, Sharon and I intentionally concentrated on reclaiming our former and inactive members, as well as establishing contact with those we could not have known, such as those who had moved to our area without initiating involvement with the church. We mailed a request to every church in our conference and to every conference in North America requesting help in identifying individuals in our metropolitan area who no longer participated in church activities. In just a few weeks, we received the names of over 200 such individuals to whom we prioritized low-key, encouraging spiritual nurture. We focused our energies and resources toward those whose lives were once united in fellowship with the Adventist Church, and within a short time, we experienced more than four dozen individuals who had returned to our church.

God loves the missing! One of the clearest lessons Jesus ever taught was our heavenly Father's concern for those missing from the fellowship of believers. Luke 15 records three different stories that demonstrate this point—the missing sheep, the missing coin, and the missing son. Interestingly, each story tells a different path by which someone ends up among the missing, often without even realizing their situation. The sheep wandered off alone. The coin never left the premises but remained separated. The prodigal son deliberately chose to leave in rebellion and ended up alone.

While we diligently search for missing and former members and collect names and accurate addresses, remember that some, much like the story of the coin, might remain in our midst, yet alone. If you think of someone like this whom you know, why not give them a telephone call right now, and let them know they are missed. Never underestimate how much influence your personal contact might have.

And in my congregation's weekly newsletter that we targeted to hundreds of readers beyond our active membership, I wrote the following: "If you are reading this and feel all alone, please know that our intent is stronger than our follow-through in too many cases. This is your personal invitation. We want you back to a far greater extent than we are capable of expressing. God's love for you is even greater than our concern. Please don't wait for someone to call you! Give us a call! Better yet, come rejoice with us in renewed fellowship!" The very next Sabbath, a family showed up at church and stated, "We understand you're looking for us—we have not attended church in over twenty years."

How to reclaim. Nine principles for reclaiming those who are missing from fellowship are outlined in Luke 15:

1. Count. The good shepherd knew that one sheep was missing because he kept careful count on those who were with him. Direct your elders to work with you in spiritually nurturing every member.

2. Risk. The shepherd left the ninty-nine sheep exposed to danger in the wild places as he went searching for the one who was missing. He risked the group's security and convenience for the one most in need! Prioritize.

3. Labor. When the homemaker discovered her coin was missing, she worked long and diligently. Nothing of value comes easily! This parable also expresses God's intention for all members to be represented in ministry. Jesus framed the Divine Sweeper as a woman.

4. Wait. Never give up! The prodigal's father had to patiently wait until his son made the choice to start back toward home. Then he ran out to greet his prodigal. God will meet any returning soul more than halfway.

5. Pray. You need not wait in idleness. Prayer is the key in the hand of faith that unlocks heaven's storehouse of blessings! When I pray for missing members, I do not pray to change God's attitude toward the lost; God changes my attitude toward the lost.

6. Love unconditionally. Never impose criteria on someone else in order for them to become recipients of your love. Express your love unreservedly! Accept them even as they stink from the pigpen; then love them into life-changing sanctified living.

7. Welcome. Joyously express your pleasure when a missing friend returns to fellowship. Make them feel wanted and welcomed! Encourage even their very first steps toward heaven. The prodigal received shoes, a ring, and a robe from his father at the moment of return.

8. Restore. Those who return have nothing to prove. The prodigal expected to be a servant; he was restored as an heir! The lost have nothing to prove to the church. We must prove our love and concern to those who have been wounded.

9. Celebrate. Make every restoration a joyous occasion. All heaven rejoices when one individual returns. We could at least host a fellowship luncheon! What better occasion to party?

Prioritizing reclamation. Mike Jones, who possesses the unique capability of thinking like a successful pastor, which he once was, and responding like a reclaimed inactive member, which he experienced for himself, states: "If the church wants to maximize its results for . . . Evangelism, I make three suggestions. (1) Local congregations should make themselves more user-friendly, (2) evangelistic emphasis should include printing small, low-budget newspaper ads that intentionally invite inactive and former members to visit, (3) and pastors and elders should lead in planning an annual Homecoming Sabbath for those who have become inactive and missing."

What's next? Now that we've seen the potential to reconnect/reclaim/reflame inactive and former members, we must "put shoes on the process" and make a concentrated effort to reconnect relationships, reclaim fellowship, and re-flame discipleship. I recommend the following process:

1. Appoint a central site for a master list of inactive and former members (The Voice of Prophecy for North America). Other divisions can institute and develop a similar plan for their territory.
2. Publish the following announcement in every church bulletin and newsletter for six consecutive weeks: **"Searching for former and inactive Adventists.** Do you have a friend or family relative who used to be a member or active in church activities? We need their name, mail address, e-mail contact, and telephone. Each person will receive an attractively designed, sensitively written packet of materials inviting them to reestablish contact with the nearest Adventist church. Send all information to: Attention: Pastor Fred Kinsey, The Voice of Prophecy, Box 53055, Los Angeles, CA 90053 (www.vop .com/reflame)."
3. Pray for the Holy Spirit to warm the heart of every individual who will receive a gracious invitation to attend worship services and to reconnect with the church of their heritage.
4. Print the following display advertisement in the "Weekend/Entertainment" section of Friday newspapers for eight consecutive weeks. For a version which you can adapt, visit www.ministerialassociation .com and click on the Reflame logo.
5. Conduct a Love Them Back seminar for every church in which pastors

will instruct members on how best to encourage and engage with those who will return to attendance. Mike Jones recommends that this seminar include the following practical methods:

    a. Make eye contact with each visitor to your church.

    b. Add a welcome smile to your eye contact.

    c. Touch your visitors with warmth and welcome. A handshake or squeeze on the shoulder gives positive impact.

    d. Ask questions designed to open conversation. "Do you folk live around here?" (Never ask if they are "visiting," which might easily offend someone who attends regularly and believes you should already know them.)

    e. Listen to your visitors. Open-ended questions are better. "How did you come to be in this city?" or "How do you feel about our worship services?" Once you've asked, listen. Suture your mouth shut and you will learn much from what they share.

    f. Talk to your visitors. Easy conversations such as, "Good morning, my name is Jim," will get the job done. At first, strive for a friendly relationship and nothing more.

    g. Defer investigating their motive for attending or their challenges of the past. Over a period of time, they may share how they have felt wounded or became disenfranchised from the church.

    h. Feed your visitors. Food and fellowship is a powerful social component and Adventists, at their best, do this very well.

    i. Simplify your own life to take time to greet at least one or two individuals you don't know every Sabbath. These connections make high impact.

6. Restrain those who reject such training from imposing their antisocial attitudes, speculative ideas, or fanciful heresies on those who visit your church.

7. Follow Jesus' model—the only way to reach the heart and mind of seekers. "Christ's method alone will give true success in reaching the people. The Saviour mingled with men as one who desired their good. He showed His sympathy for them, ministered to their needs, and won their confidence. Then He bade them, 'Follow Me' " (*The Ministry of Healing,* 143).

8. Ask the Holy Spirit to enable you to be a loving and loveable Christian who will appropriately interact with all whom God will help us reclaim.

SECTION IV:
REACHING IN

Friend-raising

A mother asked her little boy how he liked his first day of school. "I hated it," he said. "They put me in a room full of kids all by myself." Suddenly this new scholar had discovered that he could be lonely in a crowd. Individuals who join a church in which they do not participate soon feel that they have entered a lonely crowd.

Church growth studies show three components that are essential for new members to remain within the fellowship of a church: ability to articulate their beliefs, active relationships with friends, and meaningful personal ministry. With one of these missing, the member may survive in a weakened state. If two, the new member will already be moving out of the fellowship they had readily embraced.

Tragedy. A new member without a friend is a tragedy—merely a statistic—and, far too often, this statistic becomes a reality in Seventh-day Adventist churches. While the tragedy of new members without friends concerns every denomination, Adventists have a greater challenge than most others because of unique factors surrounding the doctrinal instruction presented to potential members.

Typical recruitment of new members by Adventist evangelism has emphasized the unique theological positions of the church in comparison with "others" who either lack "full truth" or are unwilling to follow what they know. Thus, Adventists experience the theologically convicted individual who embraces the doctrinal positions of the church and sometimes joins a local congregation on the basis of theological convictions alone.

Reaction to rejection. While theological convictions remain necessary, beliefs alone are insufficient to keep new members bonded to their new congregation. Because the high level of confidence in the "truthfulness" of Adventist doctrine may not have been matched with high levels of fellowship and involvement, expectations have been dashed. As a result, new believers may well experience rejection, pain, and anger at the very moment they need love, acceptance, and forgiveness. When they experience this pain, these new members cut themselves off from committing themselves to one another.

John Savage, Methodist pastor and president of LEAD Consultants, interviewed a group of inactive members regarding their reasons for leaving the church. He noted, "Each of the 23 persons interviewed in the non-active group indicated that no one from the church had ever come to find out why they were losing interest or had dropped out. . . . One third of this group cried during the interview, indicating the intensity of unresolved feelings."[1]

Believing they are unwanted and unneeded, these new members easily develop an attitude of indifference rather than risk rejection. Ken Abraham says, "Most psychologists agree that the opposite of love is not hate; it's indifference. For example, a couple having marital problems has a better chance of reconciliation if there are feelings between them, regardless how negative or bitter those feelings are. But if the couple is indifferent in their feelings, it will take serious, long-term work to recapture the love they once knew. . . . The same is true spiritually. Indifference is a killer. Even negative reactions are better than no reaction. If you sense yourself sliding toward spiritual indifference, you must take radical corrective action immediately!"[2]

Reaction to reaction. However, rather than recognizing their own acts of abandonment or the subsequent reaction of indifference by new members, longer-term members may conclude that the new member's process of indoctrination was insufficient and that this is the cause of their apostasy.

Furthermore, those pastors or members whose energies are directed to ongoing recruitment of new members are labeled as interested only in "numbers." Such destructive blame-placing negates the very mandate of the gospel commission to take the good news to every creature under heaven.

People are no longer numbers when we love them, value them, pray for and with them, and minister to them. Bailey Smith recounts the story of a Sunday School teacher who responded to a criticism of numbers with determination to emphasize quality. Next week he arrived at class to discover several of his youngsters missing. Then his love for them and concern for their souls led him on an all-out effort to get them back to class. He concluded, "Shall we strive for numbers—Yes, O Yes! When it is my boys, let's have numbers—all eleven of them!"[3]

Numbers, then, are important only because they represent individuals who need to be reached for Christ. In fact, when we understand numbers from this perspective, we realize that an individual remains only a number until someone becomes their friend and takes a personal interest. Making friends becomes not only a much-needed and excellent method of assimilating new members but also an effective evangelistic strategy.

1. John S. Savage, *The Apathetic and Bored Church Member* (Reynoldsburg, Ohio: LEAD Consultants, 1981), 57.

2. Ken Abraham, *The Disillusioned Christian* (San Bernardino, Calif.: Here's Life Publishers, 1991), 127.

3. Bailey Smith, *Real Evangelism* (Nashville, Tenn.: Thomas Nelson, 1999), 123.

Doing Church Like a Pub

Should you try making your church more like a tavern? Bruce Larson describes how the neighborhood bar becomes the substitute for the church in meeting the needs of unchurched individuals who are longing for friends: "It's an imitation, dispensing liquor instead of grace, escape rather than reality, but it is a permissive, accepting, and inclusive fellowship. It is unshockable. It is democratic. You can tell people secrets and they usually don't tell others or even want to. The bar flourishes, not because most people are alcoholics, but because God has put into the human heart the desire to know and be known, to love and be loved, and so many seek a counterfeit at the price of a few beers."[1]

If this need for friendship is essential in getting decisions, it is equally vital in keeping new converts attached to the body, both in emotional as well as physical proximity. Jerry Cook says there are three guarantees from the church that people must have before they will risk becoming open enough to receive the healing that brings spiritual maturity and wholeness. First, the guarantee that they will *always* be loved—under every circumstance—with no exception. Second, that they will be totally accepted, without reservation. Third, that no matter how miserably they fail or how blatantly they sin, unreserved forgiveness is theirs for the asking.[2]

The first and second of these guarantees are crucial in the impact of friendship for new members. A friend will love a friend and accept that person for who they are—warts and all! A friend will seldom do this for a stranger. Strangers will find little acceptance, little love, and virtually no forgiveness from a group of people who do not know them.

Furthermore, no matter how theologically persuaded new members are of the doctrinal positions of their new church, without friendship it is nearly impossible to remain in fellowship. When new members are recruited on the basis of doctrine alone, without fellowship as a strong and accompanying reality, we set both ourselves and the new members up for failure.

Rather than assuring that new believers either already have friends or gain

---

1. Harvie M. Conn, *Evangelism: Doing Justice and Preaching Grace* (Grand Rapids, Mich.: Zondervan, 1982), 29, 30.
2. Jerry Cook and Stanley C. Baldwin, *Love, Acceptance and Forgiveness* (Ventura, Calif.: Regal Books, 1979), 11.

new friends within the congregation, members often adopt a "holier than thou" attitude that excludes people at the very moment they most need inclusion. As Christians we are rightfully concerned for our unsaved loved ones. Perhaps we should show equal concern for our unloved saved ones.[3]

Applying Cook's first step to this issue of "having friends within the church," notice what he says: "Love means accepting people the way they are for Jesus' sake. Jesus hung around with sinners and if we're too holy to allow people to blow smoke in our faces, then we're holier than Jesus was. He didn't isolate Himself in the synagogue. In fact, He mixed with sinners so much that the self-righteous got upset about it. 'He's friendly with some very questionable people,' they said. And Jesus replied, 'Yes, because I didn't come to minister to you religious leaders. I came to call sinners to repentance.' Isn't that fantastic? Jesus spent His time with dirty, filthy, stinking sinners. And when those kinds of people find someone who will love and accept them, you won't be able to keep them away!"[4]

This is the very essence of discipling! This is the very process of nurturing new members to the point of fruit-bearing maturity, and the best "first fruit" they can bear will be extending love, acceptance, forgiveness, and friendship with another new believer. "Pastors are not obligated to get people to heaven. That's the work of Jesus. A pastor's obligation to people is first to love and accept and forgive them, and second, to bring them to ministry readiness by teaching them to do the same."[5]

And even this emphasis on extending forgiveness and acceptance relates directly back to articulating the doctrines—the most essential one being salvation by grace through faith in Christ Jesus. The Adventist Church needs continually to relearn that Jesus accepts us—although our lives have much that offends His holiness. Righteousness by faith in His merits says that His acceptance of us does not imply approval of our misbehavior, but rather it shows love that will transcend our shortcomings and transform our behavior into His likeness if we will only allow sufficient time to interact with Him as "a friend who sticks closer than a brother" (Proverbs 18:24, NIV)! If we, then, are acceptable to Jesus despite our lack, how could we dare reject others?

---

3. Conn, 29.

4. Robert Tuttle Jr., *Someone Out There Needs Me* (Grand Rapids, Mich.: Zondervan, 1983), 103.

5. Cook and Baldwin, 15.

Belonging

Psychologist Abraham Maslow's hierarchy of needs demonstrates that once a person moves beyond assuring the essentials to sustain life and safety, the next priority is to "belong." Further, the more change or trauma individuals have experienced, the greater their likely need for a new "reference group identification." For new church members the need to belong is essential.[1]

Thus, congregations should intentionally establish new fellowship groups as membership expands. This will enable people to continue to feel a part of the fellowship family even as the church grows, allow the church to grow without major resistance, provide the setting in which people are tied into the Word of God, and help with the assimilation of new members.[2]

The probability of new members becoming actively involved is directly tied to the number of friends that they develop soon after joining the church. Flavil Yeakley interviewed fifty new members who had become actively incorporated into the life of the church as well as fifty recent converts who had dropped out. The more quickly new members formed personal relationships within the congregation, the more likely they were to become active and involved. The converts who stayed had developed an average of more than seven new friends in the church. Those who dropped out could identify an average of fewer than two.[3]

Another study asked two questions of those who had recently departed: (1) Why did they drop out? The answer regularly given was, "Did not feel part of the group." (2) What would most influence their choice of a new church home? Nearly 75 percent responded with "friendliness of the people."[4]

Members in the churches from which these new members dropped out most likely did not consider themselves unfriendly. New members are not necessarily overtly rejected. Quite often there is a superficial level of friendliness. In fact, most congregations would be shocked if they were described as unfriendly.

Friendliness is different, however, from being friend-seeking. Common courtesy and genteel manners will lead a group of people to act in a friendly manner. On

---

1. Flavil Yeakley, "A Profile of the New Convert: Change in Life Situation," in *The Pastor's Church Growth Handbook,* vol. 2, eds. Win Arn and Charles Arn, (Pasadena, Calif.: Institute of American Church Growth, 1979), 31.

2. Kent R. Hunter, *Foundations for Church Growth* (New Haven, Mo.: Leader Publishing Co., 1973), 155.

3. *The Pastor's Church Growth Handbook,* vol. 2, 179.

4. Ibid.

the other hand, the real message that may be conveyed is "Please don't bother me with depth beyond superficial greeting." One new member in my former congregation stated, "I get the real impression that when someone asks how I'm doing they really don't want to know and would be shocked if I even attempted to tell them. They are expressing a friendly greeting, but they don't want to be my friend."

We should not be surprised if new members reject superficial courtesy offered in lieu of genuine friendship. As Ken Abraham observed: "The opposite of love is not hate; it's indifference."[5]

With regard to nurturing people into the life of the body, too many of our churches are better in form than in reality. We say the right things, but we don't provide loving, supportive relationships to back up our words. We may think we are friendly while, in fact, guests or new members do not sense a loving atmosphere at all.

Nelson Annan suggests a six-step approach toward nurturing friendship-building, inclusive relationships:

1. Communicate love. Some leaders may be strong in organizing, teaching, and leading committee meetings, but weak when it comes to relating to people. Leaders must not only love the flock, but effectively communicate that love.

2. Preach and teach love. Challenging the church to grow in love for God, for one another, and for the world around them is the pastor's privilege and responsibility.

3. Emphasize friendliness and warmth. People-oriented members who smile, love to talk, and remember names should be trained to greet visitors and intentionally nurture new believers.

4. Follow up first-time visitors. Cultivate friendships with guests; extend lunch invitations; telephone to express pleasure for their visit; mail a warm note to encourage return attendance; make a personal visit to build the bridge of friendship and, possibly, to share the gospel.

5. Broaden internal groups to make new people feel like they belong. Newcomers should be surrounded with warmth and made to feel welcome. Additionally, this atmosphere must be genuine or it quickly will be detected as artificial.

6. Strengthen and increase social events. In loving churches people spend time together outside of the church building. In order to build relationships, more time is needed than ten minutes before or after meetings. Create unique ways to bring dozens of people together to play and laugh, to work and serve, and to learn and pray together.[6]

Your objective is for people to say of your congregation, "This is where I belong!"

---

5. Ken Abraham, *The Disillusioned Christian* (San Bernardino, Calif.: Here's Life Publishers, 1991), 127.

6. Nelson Annan, *More People: Is Church Growth Worth It?* (Wheaton, Ill.: Harold Shaw Publishers, 1987), 37–40.

Dangerous Communalism

If the dissemination of information alone were sufficient to accomplish conversion, then Seventh-day Adventists, of all people, ought to be spiritual giants. With our numerous publishing ventures and worldwide network of literature evangelists, the Adventist Church is the best thing that has happened to paper since the government talked people into taking it for money.

The ability to articulate personal beliefs—to have a theological basis for a belief system and to understand its biblical focus—is essential. But knowledge alone is insufficient. Perhaps this has been the great lack in Adventist evangelism: an over-reliance on correct theology as the essential ingredient for attracting and incorporating individuals into the church without the appropriate regard for the sociological factors of friendship and involvement that must also accompany doctrinal understanding.

Adventists prize the truth. In fact, our love of theological correctness has been historically expressed with this very phrase: "the truth." The phrase was code to describe the entire subcultural phenomena of the church. Our pride in theological accuracy and orthodoxy, combined with a distinctively conservative lifestyle, has often produced a closed society into which we ostensibly welcome new believers but, practically, make it difficult for them to join.

Too often, Adventists have fostered *communalism* that John Stott describes as a "disastrous development." He refers to it as "the rise of a Christian community which, instead of being scattered throughout the non-Christian community as salt and light, becomes isolated from it as a distinct cultural entity on its own."[1]

This is evidenced by numerous Adventist communities that have sprung up around educational institutions, publishing houses, medical facilities, organizational headquarters, or other Adventist entities. Now all is not bad in these communities. There is much to recommend—the pleasant atmosphere, the safe, secure environment, and the separation from "worldly influences" that such communities provide.

However, to the extent that such communities (whether Berrien Springs, Collegedale, Cooranbong, Salisbury Park, or Stanborough Park, etc., as present-day offspring of Battle Creek and Takoma Park) fail to integrate Adventist

---

1. John R. W. Stott, *Christian Mission in the Modern World* (Downers Grove, Ill.: InterVarsity Press, 1975), 119.

believers into the life and worldview of those to whom they minister, we have added to an isolationist "communalism" more than we have preserved piety. Or worse, we have actually come to equate piety with isolationism. As one wag said it, "Adventists are like fertilizer. Spread 'em around, they do a lot of good. Pile 'em together, they stink!"

Impious humor aside, however, the very survival of Adventist growth among indigenous Western population groups may depend upon our ability to break out of this communalism. Donald McGavran and Win Arn discuss the history of the Swedish Baptists in North America, who grew chiefly among Swedes until the late 1930s when they grasped new vision and realized they were living in the midst of multitudes of unreached people who were not Swedish Americans. They resolved to cease concentrating on just those of Swedish background and to win individuals from all backgrounds. They grew from forty thousand in 1940 to more than one hundred thousand in 1976, and projected that they would double again within the next ten years.[2]

Adventist Church growth is changing rapidly. The movement was founded in the United States among an Anglo constituency and was for many years largely Anglo and, for the most part, middle-class. Speaking to Adventists about their church growth in North America, Carl George says, "your reports show Adventist growth going up year-by-year, but studying those reports carefully shows that your best growth is not occurring in the Anglo world, but among third world minorities. I don't see anything wrong with that at all. I think it is wonderful that you are extending the gospel beyond the Anglo parts of society."[3]

However, with regard to this issue of communalism, Carl George identifies problems that will prevent additional growth for Adventists: "nor should this plateauing of Anglo growth be viewed as a failure for the church. The white populations of North America have changed. Anglos, who showed the greatest potential for Adventist growth until 40 or 50 years ago, no longer present a recruitable target, at least by your current methodologies. Part of this can be attributed to lifestyle changes in America. Part can be attributed to the fact you segregate your children in Adventist schools, diminishing your contact with Gentiles."[4]

At a time when first world church growth has virtually halted, we continue to "communalize" at our own peril. Furthermore, even if it were successful, "communalism" is not biblical. Stott correctly points out that the place for the

---

2. Donald A. McGavran and Winfield C. Arn, *Ten Steps for Church Growth* (N.Y.: Harper and Row, 1977), 81.

3. Carl George, *Empty Pews, Empty Streets* (Columbia, Md.: Columbia Union Conference of Seventh-day Adventists, 1988), 50, 51.

4. Ibid.

converted individual is back in the world. "Conversion must not take the convert out of the world but rather send him back into it, the same person in the world, and yet a new person with new convictions and new standards."[5]

Imagine! Godly people living in the midst of an ungodly environment. Salt, flavoring and preserving; light, illuminating and warming. That is discipleship!

---

5. McGavran and Arn, 121.

Teaching That Takes Hold

Our Adventist sense of mission and our self-image as the *faithful remnant* drive us to evangelize the world with a last-day message aimed at "preparing a people ready to meet the Lord." Therefore, accurate understanding of prophecy, careful delineation of doctrine, and specific application of standards have been essential in our process of instructing new believers.

While we desire great numbers of new believers who become truly grounded disciples, a *quantity versus quality* debate sometimes has been fueled by those who believe insufficient preparation has preceded baptism. Those concerned that numbers have become the primary objective stress the need for less quantity and more quality. Miscomprehension of a remnant concept has contributed to this debate. While there is clear biblical basis for remnant theology—God's faithful followers in an age of overwhelming secularism and evil—this must never be used to justify lack of growth.

Here's the danger: If such a remnant view becomes directed toward justifying lack of growth, not only might we excuse little growth, we actually might glorify declining numbers as quality over quantity. Donald McGavran says, "Remnant theology proves attractive. A glorification of littleness prevails, in which to be small is to be holy. Slow growth is adjudged good growth." He points out various slogans which give false support to this type of remnant theology:

- The tiny minority suffering for its belief is the true church.
- To create this minority is the highest success known to missions.
- The persecuted church—the church under the Cross—is the true church.
- The power of a small group of individuals, with God, must never be underestimated.
- The creative minority is what the church must ever strive to be.[1]

In general, Adventists today would reject a view which stresses smallness in favor of a *triumphant remnant* concept. However, we might embrace an equally dangerous "remnant" theology of exclusivity or superiority based on a knowledge

---

1. Donald A. McGavran, *Understanding Church Growth* (Grand Rapids, Mich.: Eerdmans, 1980), 168.

of "truth" because we want our new members to be on the inside of this *truth track*. Typically, we expect new believers to have been instructed thoroughly in all points of doctrine—twenty-eight fundamental points, to be exact. Furthermore, we expect not only that the information has been conveyed and comprehended, we also want it to be operative within the behavior of the individual at the occasion of baptism.

Of course, there is nothing wrong with adequate instruction or thorough preparation of candidates for church membership. The perils of a casual acknowledgment of the gospel without a corresponding impact on the life of the believer are so abundantly visible in our denomination, and others as well, that no serious challenge could be sustained which calls for less thorough biblical instruction of new believers. In fact, just the opposite is needed—more thorough and in-depth teaching. Teaching that takes hold!

Jo Lewis and Gordon Palmer demonstrate that "core" spiritual knowledge is lacking in the American society that prides itself on being *Christian*. They cite a twenty-year-old Gallup poll that found many professing believers woefully ignorant about basic facts of Christianity. For example, 85 percent of Americans assent to the validity of the Ten Commandments and believe that someday everyone will answer to God for how they have obeyed or disobeyed them. Unbelievably, however, these same people don't know what the Ten Commandments state. Only a few can name as many as five and, of course, even fewer obey them.[2]

Worst of all, Gallup found that evangelical Christians are little better than the general populace. "Young people today know Genesis as the name of a rock band or a planetary project in a *Star Trek* film, but not as the first book of the Bible. They know Pepsi and the new generation, but not heaven and the everlasting generation; *L.A. Law*, but not God's law. They know who makes 240Zs but not the Alpha and Omega who made them. They know Nike and the winning team, but not victory in Jesus. They know how to look at *Days of Our Lives,* but not how to look into the days of their lives."[3]

Two decades later, the situation is no better. Timothy Renick's recent review of current literature, "Dumbed Down," demonstrates the relentless decline of basic biblical understanding among even professing believers. He says, "America has become a nation that is at once deeply religious and profoundly ignorant about religion."[4]

Real church growth refers not merely to an outer measurable expansion, but also to an inner experience within the body of Christ. "But grow in the

---

2. Jo H. Lewis and Gordon A. Palmer, *What Every Christian Should Know* (Wheaton, Ill.: Victor Books, 1989), 15.

3. Ibid., 74.

4. Timothy Renick, "Dumbed Down," *Christian Century,* September 4, 2007, 26.

grace and knowledge of our Lord and Savior Jesus Christ" (2 Peter 3:18, NIV). We must move beyond information to lifestyle.

Additional information alone is not the key. We need instruction, but we need more instruction in righteousness. We need more thorough spiritual and practical application as well as intellectual indoctrination for new believers. This is one of the ingredients of discipleship—perhaps the most basic.

Quit Now!

During my first year of ministry, I became known as the Stop-Smoking Bishop of Tampa Bay, Florida, thanks to our overwhelming success as we helped people quit.

When an elder in my congregation insisted that I partner with him in presenting a 5-Day Plan to Stop Smoking, I reluctantly agreed and offered to contact the local hospital to sponsor the event. "No," he replied. "Let's present it right here in our own church facility."

I thought we were doomed to failure, but "Dr. Dave" and the Holy Spirit knew better than I. We registered about a dozen attendees, one of whom was the public relations director for WFLA, the NBC radio affiliate. Not only was he successful, he became an enthusiastic promoter of cigarette cancellation and recorded several dozen spot announcements that aired three times per hour every day for a month. Overnight, both Dr. Dave and I, along with all the area churches, became famous for helping Tampa kick the habit. Newspapers and other media reported the story, and within days we were registering up to 200 people at any location where we offered the famous 5-Day Plan—and at $15.00 per registration, we were making money while doing good!

Ministry magazine editor Nikolaus Satelmajer used the same program in metro New York and even taught the plan on the commuter trains in specially designated "stop smoking cars." Again, the enormous publicity put the church "on the map."

After years of success, coupled with dozens of other commercial and public service programs by various organizations, some good progress has been achieved in reducing the percentage of smokers in North America. However, the global use of tobacco continues to be one of the most serious health and moral problems confronting humanity. I can think of no more gracious service than for a congregation to offer its community such real, practical assistance to those encumbered with the tobacco habit.

Disinterested benevolence. Your community will be impressed to see your church offering practical help with a real social, health, and moral challenge. Civic, medical, and educational entities will partner with you in this venture.

Fresh, updated materials. Contact your local conference for the *Quit Now!* materials. They are international in scope, creative in design, yet still very personalized to assist presenters in helping participants achieve success. Leadership of a *Quit Now!* program does not require a medical background. Pastors, teachers, and others in helping or leadership positions can easily adapt the instruction materials for their own use.

Simple tools. The program still relies on very basic, easy-to-follow principles for success. PowerPoint presentations and redesigned formats emphasize the value of choice, as well as the importance of water, exercise, nutrition, replacement alternatives, group support, and individualized "buddy" attention.

Financially feasible. Materials—both for group facilitators and individual attendees—are affordable. In fact, with a modest registration fee (remember that people value something for which they must invest some payment), you will likely cover all your expenses for supplies and advertising. Today, Medicare even allows reimbursement for tobacco cessation programs.

Follow-through friend-raising. Even more important than any financial "break even" is the reward of raising friends for your congregation. Through the years I have helped dozens of individuals who call me "their pastor" because I assisted them in achieving their goals. I have also discovered the value of offering ongoing small group activities for fellowship, study, and encouragement to "stay quit."

Utilize public awareness. The world's No-Tobacco Day each May and the Great American Smokeout each November offer opportunities to enhance awareness. Television and print advertising, as well as cancer and health societies, will enlist local sponsors to enhance your effectiveness.

Seize initiative. Churches should remain at the forefront in offering help to curb this plague. Amazingly, the very purveyors of tobacco products now attempt to position themselves as helping parents prevent their children from smoking even as they seek to enslave youngsters in addiction.

Try it! Your success will surprise you. God's power will accompany you. Your community will praise you. Your Lord will reward you. You can make a real difference for your community.

Not Quite Christians

Exciting and dynamic! More than 43,000 new members had been added to the church in the previous year. What rejoicing in the glad news of baptisms with such an abundant inflow of new members that equaled a completely new conference.

Unfortunately, however, the statistical report of great membership growth was not matched by other measurable faithfulness factors such as worship attendance or church finances. For the year following all these new accessions, per capita tithe income had not increased by one penny in the same territory.

When I queried this disparity of statistics, one leader suggested that it is unfair to evaluate their weak economy in comparison to a "healthy Western economy." My response remains, "Ten percent of even a very weak economy stays at ten percent. God does not ask for tithe of a United States dollar; He asks for faithfulness in tithing the currency of wherever believers live."

George Gallup observes, "Many Americans belong to the not quite Christian category: . . . They want the fruits or reward of faith, but seem to dodge the responsibilities and obligations. They say that they are Christian but often without a visible connection to a congregation or religious fellowship. The major challenge appears to be . . . how to guide men and women into becoming mature Christian personalities."[1]

Discipleship, then, involves the whole process of initial instruction (pre-baptism), welcoming the new member into the community (at baptism, for Adventists), and teaching them to observe all things (post-baptism).

The ongoing discussion, of course, is, "How much and what type of instruction is to precede baptism?" Peter Wagner ably addresses this issue of pre-baptismal instruction versus post-baptismal development in an excellent chapter titled, "The Gospel, Conversion, and Ethical Awareness," in his book *Church Growth and the Whole Gospel.*

There is some risk in keeping the ethical content of discipling to a minimum in preaching free grace. But to me there seems a greater risk in prematurely trying to uproot the tares and destroying some of the wheat in the process. I know of many evangelists who do not insist, as

---

1. George Gallup, Jr., and David Poling, *The Search for America's Faith* (Nashville: Abingdon, 1980), 42, 43.

a prerequisite to salvation, that unbelievers agree to tithe their income. But after they become Christians they learn that their new Lord expects them to tithe their income. This is not bothersome to the average Christian. Initial repentance and conversion means turning to Christ as the Lord of life, and when, over a lifetime of discipleship, the Lord speaks and brings new requirements to their attention, they are cordially accepted. Taking the step of tithing is an advance in Christian obedience, more a part of perfecting than of discipling.[2]

This perfecting role becomes the privilege and duty of the church. "A perfecting which lifts educational attainments, increases earning ability, heightens conscience as to social justice, and decreases concern to win kindred to eternal life, betrays the Gospel. High secular and cultural attainments must not be mistaken for dedication to Christ."[3]

When does this perfecting role occur in the life of the new believer? "Undisciplined pagan multitudes must be 'added to the Lord' before they can be perfected. The church exists not for herself but for the world. She has been saved in order to save others. She always has a twofold task: winning men to Christ and growing in grace. While these tasks overlap, they are distinct."[4]

An "instruction in righteousness" exists as necessary to post-baptism as surely as there are essentials that need to be accepted and believed prior to baptism. George Hunter offers these conclusions from a study of about four thousand converts in India: "Their post-baptismal training was more influential in whether they remained and grew in the Christian community than even the motives which originally attracted them to Christianity."[5]

And fellowship with the community of believers will have its impact. Information may be imperfectly communicated, but in the long run what is caught by association with fellow believers may be more important than what is taught as far as discipleship is concerned. This "teaching" cannot be limited to merely intellectual knowledge, but must be implemented into the life. This describes applied theology—applied in the daily Christian walk.

Bill Hull says that the Greek word for disciple—*mathetes*—means learner, pupil, someone who learns by following. "The word implies an intellectual process that directly affects the lifestyle of a person."[6] It also anticipates a

---

2. C. Peter Wagner, *Church Growth and the Whole Gospel* (San Francisco: Harper & Row, 1981), 140.

3. Ibid.

4. Ibid.

5. George G. Hunter III, *The Contagious Congregation: Frontiers in Evangelism and Church Growth* (Nashville: Abingdon, 1979), 143.

6. Bill Hull, *Jesus Christ Disciple Maker* (Old Tappan, N.J.: Fleming H. Revell Co., 1978), 10.

growing in faith—a completion, sanctifying process by which not-quite Christians become functioning disciples within the body. Juan Carlos Ortiz points out that this application of discipleship must be conveyed by more than intellectual instruction. "In a discipleship relationship I do not teach the other person to know what I know, rather I teach him to become what I am. Discipleship then is not a communication of knowledge but a communication of life and spirit."[7]

---

7. Michael Harper, *Let My People Grow* (Plainfield, N.J.: Logos International, 1977), 152.

Visitation Expectation

Every pastor ought to visit the members. Every visit ought not be made by the pastor. These two statements summarize the crux of overwrought expectations for pastoral visitation. Another denominational magazine recently opined on the insensitivity of shepherds who published instructions in their bulletin for members to request pastoral visits.

Systematic, consistent visitation of church members does need to occur, and members have reasonable expectations that such pastoral visitation will occur.

However, members have unreasonable expectations if they believe the pastors should personally perform the visitation process that rightly belongs within the assignment of the local church elders and other laity leadership.

For example, in my last pastoral assignment, I could have made a full-time career out of circulating among the seven or eight hospitals in our metropolis where my sick members were being treated. The circuit to just one of those hospitals—the most prestigious in the region—took over three hours from the church to a short visit at the hospital bedside and back again.

Reasonable expectation—sick members will be visited, especially when they are in the hospital. Unreasonable expectation—the pastor will personally do that visitation. An irate member complained that she had been hospitalized, and I had failed to visit her. I responded, "But you did receive a pastoral visit from two of the elders who reported to me of your progress." When she retorted, "But you did not visit," I recalled and repeated the statement I had learned from a wise, older pastor. "Sister, let us right now offer a prayer of thanksgiving that you were not so ill that they had to call for me to visit. You do not want to become that sick." In that same pastorate, I surveyed each member right at the beginning of my tenure. Upon analysis, one of the multiple-choice questions produced interesting insight. The question:

How would you like to receive pastoral visits?
__ Drop in anytime.
__ By appointment only.
__ Only when I request a visit.

The surprising result was the age demographic for the various respondents. The first option was primarily selected by retirees over age sixty-five. The "By appointment only" option was most typically the response of mid-career members, ages forty to sixty-five. The "Only when requested" group was heavily weighted to the "under forty" group, many of them young adults and over-extended parents of small children.

I wonder if the responses would follow the same age/schedule track if the congregation were surveyed again today. I believe that expectations would shift along with the changed circumstances of life. The analysis of that survey encouraged me to reclassify pastoral visitation into several categories of need and responsibility.

Proactive visitation. We enlarged our board of elders and divided the congregation into groups for which the laity leaders were responsible for regular visitation on behalf of the pastoral team.

Our elders were always to visit with a partner. As pastor, I would rotate among the elders and thus could visit some of the members from time to time while assuring that all the members would be routinely visited over the course of the year.

Reactive visitation. Family crisis such as death, traumatic illness and anointing, or unexpected challenges received a higher priority in which our elders knew to involve the pastor in the visitation process. Such reactive visits could also come at joyous times such as wedding preparations, birth and child dedications, graduation celebrations, or home dedications. Remember how much ministry Jesus accomplished at banquets, funerals, and social gatherings.

"Deactive" visitation. If permitted, emotionally unstable individuals would monopolize nearly all of the pastor's time. Such members must have specific limitations set or nothing else could be accomplished beyond allowing them to vent their frustrations or expound fanciful theological theories.

When someone asks to relate their long, involved story, I always respond: "I can give you ten minutes now or a half-hour next week if you wish to write all the information out so that I can read and understand your thinking in advance." My busy schedule forces them to prioritize or seek other outlets.

Creative visitation. Much of my personal visitation was designed around engaging people whose circumstances could make an "influence contribution" to the church. For example, praying with police officers, firefighters, judges, and city officials. I asked my members to introduce me to their business associates, neighbors, and friends whose influence would positively impact the church. I invested time and energy in relationships with pastors of all denominations and unchurched associates of my leaders.

Instructive visitation. The most delightful visitation for me develops people for spiritual growth, preparation for baptism and church membership, pre-marital counseling, leadership development, and creative visioning in areas where the church can expand.

Where have all the shepherds gone? Because they are typically overworked, I hope they have gone for some vacation time, especially if they have the assurance that proper planning provides consistent visitation for their members.

Visitation Revisited

We pastors seldom visit too much. Only once did I know a pastor who *overvisited*—from first thing every morning until too late into the evening. His colleagues often repeated jokes about his reputation for visiting at such odd hours, calling him a "visiting fool." His members called him something else—"our best pastor ever!"

Too often, our good intentions for visiting members collide with reality in the form of overcrowded schedules, urgencies trumping essentials, insufficient time for our own families, plus inadequate planning. These encroach to the point that our performance seldom matches the expectations our members have for us or even those we expect from ourselves.

Back in the day when pastors were *required* to list cumulative visits on the monthly conference report, I was shocked one time to learn than an intern had reported nearly 200 visits for a particular month. In fact, a quick review of his previous reports showed that he seldom reported less than 100 pastoral or evangelistic visits per month. Attempting to match these extraordinary reports to his ordinary behavior, I asked about his method for achieving such grand totals. "Oh, that's easy," he responded. "Each day I meet the parents as they collect their kids from school. In just a half hour, I make at least twenty spiritual visits."

Even when members receive pastoral care, they sometimes fail to identify the spiritual nurture they have received because it may not match their expectations. A conference official once expressed frustration that his pastor had not visited his home in years except when his mother died. While this was a factual report, accuracy and reality should also indicate that this leader's heavy travel, committee, and weekend schedule left him seldom at home to receive visitation. Numbers of his colleagues, myself included, had come to his office to pray with him and encourage his effective leadership. But because these instances had not occurred at his house, he did not view such encounters as pastoral visitation. If this leader believed he had not received adequate pastoral care, imagine what members have concluded when they report, "We never see the pastor."

Another leader, facing professional discipline for misconduct, widely complained that none of his colleagues had extended pastoral care in his hour of trauma despite the reality that he had declined counsel and care from several ministers including longtime friends.

Sometimes, people refuse to be pastored. Others may fail to recognize acts that we believe express sensitive care and appropriate concern.

Beyond regularly scheduled systematic visitation of your members, which should function best as an intentionally coordinated plan by the pastor and elders together, specific instances demand pastoral visitation with an essential and clearly expressed agenda.

Serious illness. Visit a dying person to share an assuring text of Scripture, inquire about their spiritual peace with God ("How do you feel about God's assurance of personal love in your own life?"), encourage hope in Jesus' soon return, and ask if they have specific prayer requests or if they would like to be anointed. Such visits accomplish much more if they are relatively brief rather than marathon sessions. Remember, Jesus assured salvation to the thief on the cross with just a dozen words.

Hospital. When visitation occurs at a medical facility, pastors should be sensitive to prioritize the busy schedule of physicians, technicians, and therapists, as well as noting the lack of privacy if other patients share the same room. While you may appropriately offer to include another patient sharing the same room in prayer, you should anticipate that lack of privacy may make your parishioner uncomfortable with in-depth discussions of spiritual or physical issues. Always ask about a person's requests for your prayer on their behalf. Don't assume that you know. A young parent may be eager for healing and full restoration of strength, while an older saint may be longing for a quick and peaceful end to life in confident assurance of Jesus' return.

Grief. Simply being there with the family forms the most beneficial process of pastoral visitation at the time of death in a family. Your physical presence provides much more meaningful care than any words or exhortations you express. Sit quietly with the family and allow plenty of time for listening to their responses to your question, "Tell me about your loved one's life . . ." Bible promises of Jesus' return, our heavenly home, and God's promised restoration of all good things are excellent ways to assure grief-stricken families of your pastoral care. The most meaningful pastoral care I received during the hour immediately following the news of my brother's death came from a pastoral couple whom I had never met. They simply stood silently by my side, hands on my shoulder, while I made telephone calls and processed the impact of such a sudden loss.

Focused Visitation

You cannot visit all the members all the time. The reality of overcrowded schedules and overstressed ministers often leaves an awesome expectation gap between intention and reality.

In my own family, for example, immediately following the airplane crash that took my brother's life, my father complained that his pastor had failed to visit despite the reality that five pastors were in his home with him at the moment I learned of the tragedy and telephoned from halfway around the world. Only later, my father discovered that the pastor he believed had ignored his grief had been graciously guarding the crash site.

When members repeat a favorite litany, "We haven't seen our pastor in years," I always attempt to query their assertion in greater depth. "Tell me," I ask, "when did you last request your pastor to visit you?" "Have you alerted the church elders of your needs?" "What do you believe the pastor is doing while you are not being visited?" Too often, I discover that expectations are different than reality and that complaints are actually "recreational" griping. In one case, a complaining parishioner explained that it had been at least seven weeks since their pastor had been to visit. Disappointment results from members whose expectations have not been met, and reconciliation occurs only when both pastors and members more closely align their expectations with reality.

I have also discovered that increasing urbanization hinders rather than helps visitation. While it is accurate that more members may live in closer physical proximity in large cities than those in rural areas, various complexities actually deter the process of metropolitan pastoral visitation much more than the longer distances of rural areas. These complexities include traffic and transit issues, irregular work schedules, nontraditional housing arrangements, and increasing inaccessibility to high-rise buildings or gated communities.

Society also has changed expectations for timing and frequency of fellowship and nurture. I aim to correct the misperception that the perceived lack of visitation comes from either pastoral indifference or indolence. I am attempting to clarify that pastors have multiple schedule complexities that may prevent them from accomplishing what they would likely prefer to be doing. I also refuse to ever permit jokes about pastoral schedules to go unchallenged. When someone says, "I wish I had a job where I work only one day per week," I invite them to work alongside me for just one day and then report their convictions about the workload.

In fact, I believe each pastor should provide a weekly activity report during worship services. Typically, just before beginning my sermon, I relate a few events of my pastoral week so that my members understand the various items that have consumed my time and energy. At monthly board meetings, I always provide an in-depth pastoral report so that leaders grasp the complexity of pastoral responsibilities and help provide explanations to members who might complain of neglect. I also believe that pastors should understand the power of even a brief visit. In fact, I have learned that most pastoral visits can be accomplished in much less time than we might imagine. Remember, a pastoral visit need not be everlasting in order to be immortal. A short, focused visit can actually accomplish more than extended conversations that lack purpose or planning.

If possible, visit only by appointment. Signal the importance and brevity of your visit as you establish the initial contact. When you telephone, state, "My visitation partner and I are making brief visits to a number of individuals in your area. When could I schedule a fifteen minute appointment with you?"

Advance notice permits the Holy Spirit to prepare their hearts and minds for spiritual business. Upon your arrival, get right to your spiritual agenda. Inquire as to their spiritual welfare—time in Bible study and prayer. Listen carefully to their responses and then ask about their faithfulness to the Holy Spirit's leading in their lives regarding church attendance, stewardship, fellowship, and witnessing. Ask whether they have any texts or topics on which they would like to hear a sermon, whether they have family or friends whom they might invite to attend church services with them, and conclude by inviting specific requests for which you can pray as you bless their home.

Even the specifics of your questions can signal that you expect a short response. Take responsibility for focusing responses. Beware of any story that begins, "Back in 1967, . . ." and bring such rambling discourses to a quick conclusion by saying, "I wish I had time to share all these details, but I'm expected at another home in just a little while." Ask for the Holy Spirit's help and your own visitation can become more focused and your pastoral experience more personally fulfilling.

What New Believers Need

Often we neglect the sobering work of discipling in favor of going back to the much more exciting process of gathering new converts. The dazzle of public preaching, coupled with the joy of witnessing thousands baptized, makes disciple-building seem mundane and, thus, easy to neglect.

However, we neglect follow-up at our own peril and at risk to the kingdom we hope to advance. Jesus' great commission intends that newborn believers will be preserved, nurtured, and built into His body as strong disciples. All of this—the whole process—is evangelism. As Peter Wagner so eloquently reminded his church growth classes, "any scheme which separates evangelism and follow-up into distinct functions has already built into the system its own defeat."

So what do new members need? In a word, "everything." Just as a newborn totally depends upon its parents for survival, so newly born believers are totally dependent upon the church's parental role in everything necessary for their survival.

Jesus intentionally chose familiar imagery of love, family, conception, gestation, birth, development, and maturity to describe the process (evangelism must always be understood as process, not event) by which individuals are brought to belief and matured into discipleship. If we wonder what new believers need, we can simply apply what newborns need to the spiritual development of new believers.

Total care. Loving nurture, tender care, acceptance, affirmation, companionship, conversation, admiration, high-touch bonding, appreciation, security, simple food, cleaning, copious companionship, and consistent attention are vital for the survival of either babies or believers.

Discipline. Long before reasoning allows an infant to comprehend dangerous situations, a firmly worded "No!" command is essential to protect the baby from placing their hand in a fire. Such protection is essential to learning the authority of both God's Word and the responsible parent. Discipline is not harshly punitive, but protective. Abandoning a baby to its own conclusions would be destructive abuse.

Instruction. The milk of the Word is repetitive assurance of God's love, acceptance, and forgiveness; freighted not so much with information as with reassurance; taught by mentoring example, not by reasoned logic. Infants learn to walk, not by a discourse on the dynamics of locomotion, but by a patterning of "walking with them" until, eventually, they take their first steps.

Education. Next, believers must be taught to think for themselves. Education is not assimilating information only. Education is learning to reason for one's self rather than merely reflecting the thoughts of others. "Why?" questions are essential in the educational steps.

Discernment. Youngsters must learn to distinguish between the genuine and clever counterfeits. When my brother John was a toddler, he drank a glass of gasoline thinking it was ginger ale. Deadly consequences were averted only by immediate intervention. Believers must be taught to test the "winds of doctrine" that are swept their way by all manner of well-meaning and ill-intentioned individuals.

Deployment. Every believer must receive a ministry assignment. Otherwise, they cannot mature and will remain perpetually immature dependents. The work of the pastor is to "work" the members.

Partnership. Those being deployed must also be partnered with experienced leaders who teach by associative example what they have experienced themselves. From the very beginning, Jesus designed a partnership role for the most effective pursuit of any good venture. It is dangerous to work alone.

Supervision. The deployed must also be closely supervised to assure their success and to correct mistakes from becoming habits. When Jesus sent His disciples two-by-two, He also brought them back together after a short time to evaluate their performance, rejoice in their successes, and instruct them for even greater achievements.

Accountability. Maturing disciples must embrace accountability both to leadership and to their fellow members.

Independence in belief or action indicates immaturity. Unwillingness to accept the counsel of the wider body disqualifies anyone.

Responsibility. As disciples mature, they will value the things that their Savior values. His priorities will be their priorities. His mission will become their mission. They will earnestly pray and diligently work to build up His church and to hasten His coming.

Reduplication. Only when the disciple is reproducing other new believers and assisting them into become disciples do you have maturity. Only then is the church's evangelistic process complete as these disciples, themselves, are effectively engaged in birthing new believers.

SECTION V:
REACHING TOGETHER

Get Back in the Closet

The news was both devastating and scandalous—a renowned pastor exposed as a longtime homosexual.

Imagine the pain, anger, frustration, and disappointment when he and his lifestyle were forced "out of the closet" into open scrutiny by the media. Like a pebble cast into still water, the scandal's expanding ripples impacted ever-widening circles.

First, there was the reality of his own sinful behavior that resulted in the abrupt termination of his career as a pastor. He had publicly preached against the gay agenda, and the court of public opinion is ruthless in its ridicule of those whose faith pretensions are not matched by their faithful performance.

Second, his own disaster was coupled with his wife's trauma as she suddenly was forced to confront her own betrayal in public—even as she discovered in the harshest way possible that, at some level, their marital relationship had been a sham for many years. Likewise, his children and extended family were thrust into the spotlight under most unfortunate circumstances.

The consequences of clergy sexual misconduct, however, do not stop with the family. Reports that rocketed into the news brought utter devastation to members who felt betrayed by their pastor's fall. Likely it may take more than a decade for members to trust pastoral leadership again.

Likewise, his pastoral colleagues—several of whom he had personally recruited to ministry or assisted in developing their pastoral/evangelistic skills—were stunned by their mentor's behavior. More than one even questioned the validity of their own call to ministry when they faced reality about the minister who had been God's agent in extending that call.

Beyond the local church, his entire denominational structure—in fact, the wider body of all Christians—experienced another blow, especially in the minds of skeptics who assume all believers are covering up some secret sin and wonder whether their conversion claims actually stand for reality. Television comedians enjoyed rousing applause as they mocked the pretenses of the notorious preacher. No wonder one of his own members responded by asking, "Why couldn't he have just stayed in the closet?"

Of course, this became a tragedy for the entire church as well as for the sinful pastor. What can we learn for the future?

Don't categorize some sins as more shameful. While it is true that public attention and church shame are more exposed in sexual sin than other sins such as thievery, prevarication, murder by gossip, or profanity, God views all sin as heinous, deserving the death penalty, and able to be overcome only by the blood of Jesus.

Don't shun the sinner. Exposed sinners, particularly pastors who rarely have adequate nurturing support systems, need to hear from their colleagues that they are still valued as individuals. Silence is our easiest escape when we are offended by a colleague's misconduct. Our silence is spiritually deadliest when a sinner yearns for a sympathetic word.

Develop a support system. I've been praying for my Adventist colleague, and I hope that he has been praying for me. We need each other's prayers. Heaven has used this pastor mightily in the past, and God may use him again to reach other individuals. Never assume you could not morally fall. Find or establish an accountability group of trusted colleagues or members who require you to discuss what you read, where you go, who you see, and how you handle the temptations you face.

Offer positive options. We must signal three things to any individual, especially to those who have betrayed the church's trust: love, acceptance, and forgiveness. Affirm heaven's love for every sinner, because no one is beyond God's grace. Express acceptance—not of the sin, but of the sinner. Remember, God's grace accepts any repentant prodigal. In the name of Jesus who forgives you, forgive others who sin. Of course, a repentant sinner must ask the Lord's forgiveness, but that first step is often prompted by some saint's personal assurance of Jesus' love and eagerness to forgive.

Get back into the closet yourself. Jesus spoke about entering our prayer closet (Matthew 6:6) and pleading with heaven. I'm convinced we need much more prayer for and much less speculation about the sinners in our midst. There, in the closet, is the location and method for victory.

Extending Your Call

"You don't remember, but twenty years ago you hired several students for some manual labor, and at the end of the project you suggested that perhaps God could call me to ministry. I had never considered the idea before, but your affirmation began the process."

Those words, spoken by a pastor, startled me. And they reaffirmed something that I have believed all along, which is that some of us reject recruiting others into ministry because of the misguided belief that a call to ministry is so mystical that we should never interfere in this highly personal, inwardly focused experience.

The fact is that a genuine call to ministry cannot be limited to an individual's own sense of God's purpose. There's more: First, along with the Spirit's impression/invitation to the individual comes the Spirit's distribution of essential gifts to accomplish the task; then comes the Spirit's conviction upon the church that the potential candidate must be set aside for specific service. If these other factors are missing, even a sincere desire does not constitute a genuine call.

Valid calls are never self-authenticated. All three elements are essential: God's personal calling to the individual, God's Holy Spirit gifting the one who is called beyond natural talent or innate capabilities (although these will certainly become enhanced within a genuine call), and God's church recognizing and affirming the work of the Spirit.

As a minister, therefore, I have the significant privilege and responsibility to seek out and recognize the potential in others. And, rather than merely awaiting a lightning strike, I can spark the flame.

Volunteers make poor candidates. Jesus personally invited each of the Twelve, except Judas. Some people overestimate their potential or mistakenly confuse the general call to discipleship (which comes to every believer) with a specific call to gospel ministry. Many others never imagine what they could accomplish, so they fail to volunteer. Seeking and recruiting potential recruits was Jesus' method for obtaining workers.

Not every recruit will accept. The rich young ruler (Luke 18:18–23) declined the same invitation that Andrew, Peter, James, and John accepted. Your expression of confidence in someone's ability may ignite their responsive mind, or they may, like the ruler, turn away.

Disciples will learn. Willingness to learn (discipleship) is more important for developing pastors than are innate capabilities. Time spent with Jesus is more productive than a theological or exegetical analysis of Jesus or His teachings.

Leaders are not born. The myth that leaders are born perpetuates mediocrity. Likewise, leaders are not made. They are not created out of nothing. Leaders are developed by other leaders.

Learning best comes through association. Potential pastors learn best from associating with godly leaders, such as pastors, teachers, local church elders— "the elect," if you will. This is why intern development is such an essential part of ministry.

Start with youngsters. Recruitment cannot begin too soon. As you discover gifted children, ask them to consider whether God might call them to His ministry. Local churches are incubators. Our congregations have an important role in developing potential pastors. By valuing and cooperating with their own pastors, they build confidence in youth who might be considering a pastoral career.

Never reject possibilities. Don't assume that you know each person's full potential. Trust the Holy Spirit to develop the most unlikely prospects into outstanding ministry candidates.

Reject false criteria. Christian churches are forbidden to use race, social status, or gender when considering who might serve God's cause (Galatians 3:26–28). Jesus' call to the Samaritan woman at the well crossed racial, social, and gender barriers in order to make her the first public evangelist (John 4:1–42)

Become a talent scout. Pastors have the privilege of serving as talent scouts. Encourage your member families to anticipate that God might use their children in ministry.

Identify successful strategies. Schools and the church should work together to reduce role expectation conflicts between the recruitment/education process (which emphasizes study, research, introspection, discussion, and reflection) and the deployment/field process (which emphasizes action, leadership, social interaction, and extroversion activities such as public speaking, administration, people skills, or visitation).

Emphasize positive contributors. Your church culture will factor strongly in whether a young person considers ministry. Preach participation in Jesus' mission. Extend opportunities for youth involvement in new ventures. Support active growth and family discipleship. Express your own joy in hearing and speaking God's Word as well as your reward in seeing others saved to God's kingdom.

Leadership: A New Start for Your Ministry

Most pastors are too busy; the majority carries a far heavier load than God intends. Consider a new approach that will renew your ministry to the extent you invest your energies in expanding your leadership team as the model and measure of pastoral success.

Resign your position as the one who directs and implements all ministry functions. Your assignment does not include doing the work of ministry. You are called to put your members to work doing ministry.

Renew your ministry by doing less and expecting more from others. Leading your elders to accomplish the Lord's will enables your own ministry to accomplish far more than you ever dreamed.

Reconfirm your responsibility not to do everything—a burnout guarantee. Instead, determine to expand your ministry base by increasing the number of individuals assigned to and involved in your ministry. Recruit new elders who will join with you in accomplishing heaven's goals for your ministry. From the very beginning Jesus envisioned His kingdom moving forward by teams. His own method involved bringing a small group of leaders together and then deploying them in pairs as He sent them out.

Reject volunteer leaders. Typically those who offer their services are full of uneducated enthusiasm but are not prepared for the costs of long-term service. Among Jesus' disciples, only Judas volunteered. The others were personally recruited by the Lord.

Remember your own origins. If the potential leaders you recruit appear to lack what ministry needs, reflect on how God has led in your own life. I recently fellowshiped anew with two successful pastors who once had been new converts and later were elected as elders before studying for ministry. Potential is often easily overlooked.

Rejuvenate your own spirit by sharing the load with other dedicated leaders, men and women, whom God will call to work alongside you. A team approach of pastor and elders cooperating together will breathe new strength into your own vision.

Recognize innate talents and gifts that God can use. Match assignments for newly recruited elders to their own talents and interests in order to multiply their effective service. Avoid forcing introverts into public, upfront roles or shutting people persons away from visitation and personal interaction.

Require specific commitments from each elder whom you recruit. Do not generalize. Define specific responsibilities with well-written job expectations. Include an estimate of the minimum hours per week that will be necessary to perform the tasks. Ask whether they are able and willing to commit.

Release those whom you elect to accomplish their assigned tasks. They may work differently than you. But remember: while they are engaged, you will be freed to pursue different objectives.

Risk that these tasks may not be performed with the same skill level you might bring. Of course, the even greater ego risk comes from realizing that your elders might do a better job.

Resource your laity leaders to do their assignments. They may need training or equipment. They will surely need mentoring. Whatever the church invests will be repaid in more effective service.

Reference helpful tools in training your elders. Specific resources such as *The Church Manual, Elder's Handbook, Minister's Handbook,* and Ellen White's *Pastoral Ministry* should form a basic library for every laity leader (order at www.ministerialassociation.com).

Relate to your elders so that each becomes part of the larger team with a desire and commitment to achieve the group's objectives. When Jesus trained His own disciples, He invested quality time in doing ministry with them, in their presence, before He sent them out two-by-two.

Replicate your own pastoral care in the ministry of your elders. Provide them church business cards so that when they visit hospitals, contact potential converts, assist members, or engage in church business they are designated as "the pastoral team."

Respect the scriptural view of the priesthood of all believers. The greater your own confidence in the role of laity leaders, the greater will be their individual ministry performance.

Review your group's goals, accomplishments, and challenges in regularly scheduled meetings with your leadership team. Help each elder understand that their contribution will set a higher standard for the church.

Revitalize and retool your own pastoral skills with the extra time you gain from effectively utilizing elders.

Rejoice when your leadership becomes reduplicated in the lives and work of your elders.

What Pastors Owe Their Associate Leaders

Whether the church has a large membership with a pastoral staff or is a small church with a pastor and local church elders, a team effort becomes necessary to have a successful ministry. Although they are colleagues in sharing the gospel, the pastor[1] assumes the lead in fulfilling the Great Commission in that particular area of God's vineyard. In order to effectively labor, pastors must place their associates in the best possible position. What, then, do they owe those who assist them?

Trust. Associate pastors bring their own academic and specialized training with them, which prepare them for the tasks to which they have been called. Having given them their responsibilities and instructions, trust them to effectively and efficiently fulfill those areas of obligation. When you have to preach at another church, it does not matter whether the church elders who speak during the divine worship hour have degrees in theology or accounting or whether or not they are dynamic speakers. They want and need your trust. Empower them and release them to employ the spiritual gifts God has placed within them.

Equipping. Provide resources for continuing development. As possible and financially feasible, such resources can take the form of workshops (inviting others with expertise in various areas to come and train them), books and journals (such as *Ministry*), discussion forums, and many others. And don't overlook what, for many, is the most vital resource—you and your presence. Young associates especially appreciate the time you spend in mentoring them, for even the very words you speak one-on-one serve to equip them for the challenges ahead.

Direction. From the time Moses led the children of Israel through the wilderness to today, leadership has been vital for the church. Although the Holy Spirit can and will directly share a vision with associate pastors and other church leaders, the lead pastor must also provide direction for the church. Pastors who exhibit such leadership qualities inspire confidence from their associates and the church membership at large.

Motivation. Closely connected with direction is motivation. It's one thing to point others toward the goal. It's another thing to inspire them to believe they can accomplish the task.

---

1. In using the word *pastor,* I refer to the senior pastor who has other pastors who serve on his staff or the solo pastor who has elders assisting at the local church level.

Motivation either comes from inside the person (intrinsic) or from outside the person (extrinsic). Some people merely need to know what is expected, and that is all the impetus they need. But most people, even in ministry, need to know that you, as pastor, believe in them; and that is often all the motivation they need. Tell them you have confidence in their ability to succeed— that will greatly benefit your associates.

Another source of motivation is *appreciation*. Say "Thank you," and say it often. No one wants to feel that they are merely workers in a system, but rather unique individuals, fulfilling the call that God has placed upon them.

Cooperation. Confidence in pastoral leadership is enhanced when those who assist you see that you have been or are doing the same activities you ask them to do. Associates want to know that the leaders comprehend the challenges that they themselves face.

This does not imply that the pastor can ably perform everything that the associates can; rather, that the pastor has a working familiarity with the assigned task and, more importantly, that the pastor actively works with the staff. This involves more than delegation; it involves cooperation. While Jesus delegated tasks to His disciples, He was actively involved in showing them how to fulfill those tasks, taking the lead, being the Chief Servant among the servants.

Rest. Placing too many responsibilities upon your associates—no matter how competent they are—leads to burnout. They may be willing to work long hours, but even if they are unwilling to slow down, the pastor must slow them down—requiring they take time for rest and rejuvenation. Although ministry is important, rest is equally important. And Jesus is our Example in demanding rest of His colleagues (cf. Mark 6:31).

Personal ministry. Pastors are understandably seen as shepherds to their congregations. But they also are shepherds to their associates, for ministers need ministry. Remember that your associates—whether paid or volunteers— are not mere workers in a system; rather, they are human beings first who have their own spiritual, mental, and social needs to address.

Ministry has always been, and always will be, a team effort. While the dynamic between pastor and associate exists, we are all colleagues in service to the Master, and as such, we exist to serve our congregations *and* one another. Let us work together, and in doing so, we will all grow together in Christ, rendering greater service as time goes by.

Defeating the Axis of Spiritual Evil— Part 1

In the annals of history there have been times when nations have formed an axis of evil in which their own people or other nations have suffered. Borrowing this analogy, the church faces a massive threat to the very core of our spirituality—a massive threat that relishes prejudicial differences of race, class, gender, or heritage.

As we boast that we are rich and increased with goods, having need of nothing, this spiritual axis of evil exults in our racial divisions, in our social distinctions, and in our gender discrimination of worship, fellowship, polity, and deployment of laborers. With such an intolerable status, Jesus threatens to spew us out of His mouth (Revelation 3:16).

Surely Jesus longs for His church to have progressed, after two millennia, beyond the fever of compromise, the fervor of rationalization, the histrionics of boasting, or the hysterical separations that plagued the early church.

Along with His dismay, however, God also provides the solution for victory over this evil axis. The secret of transformation for the church today has not changed—it lies in becoming God's children. This means putting on Jesus in our daily lives as much as putting Him on in our profession.

"For ye are all the children of God by faith in Christ Jesus. For as many of you as have been baptized into Christ have put on Christ. There is neither Jew nor Greek, there is neither bond nor free, there is neither male nor female: for ye are all one in Christ Jesus. And if ye be Christ's, then are ye Abraham's seed, and heirs according to the promise" (Galatians 3:26–29, KJV).

Cause-effect relationship. Did you note the process? Being baptized into Christ means putting on Christ with the consequence that we are all one. If we are in Christ, we no longer experience racial division. If we are in Christ, we no longer experience social distinction. If we are in Christ, we no longer experience gender discrimination. Paul's theology is clear. If we still exhibit such unconverted, unsanctified characteristics, then we must ponder whether we are really "in Christ." Moreover, Paul's theology demands more than lip-service acknowledgment. It demands implementation in our practice equal to affirmation in our theology.

The evil of racial division. If we are "in Christ," then racism, tribalism, pride of nation of origin, or segregation remains sinful as much today as it was when Paul admonished the churches of Galatia. Yet, in many parts of the globe, the "righteousness" of the children of darkness exceeds the righteousness—or at least the right behavior—of the children of light. In some countries, we are mandated by law not to segregate with respect to schooling, housing, employment, or citizenship rights. But when we exercise nonmandated free choice, we choose to segregate ourselves, and the hour of divine worship remains the most self-segregated hour of the entire week.

The evil of social distinction. In his article "Living by the Word: God's Choice," Stephen Fowl states, regarding the apostle James's admonitions about pandering to the wealthy and powerful, "We are much more comfortable operating in the realm of power and wealth because it seems like something we can manage for our own benefit and even for the benefit of others. The most charitable account one can offer of the actions of the characters addressed in James is that they were seeking to cultivate the favor of the rich and powerful to benefit the church and its mission" (*Christian Century,* September 5, 2006, 20). Yet, it is sobering to survey the socioeconomic status of those who populate our church boards, governance committees, and policy-creating commissions. Fowl says, "This is a bit of a puzzle. On the one hand, James is uncompromising in his assertion that making distinctions between people based on their wealth is a violation of the commandment to love your neighbor as yourself. Such distinctions work in opposition to God's plan of choosing 'the poorer of the world to be rich in faith and heirs of the kingdom' " (Ibid.).

The evil of gender discrimination. Like the other evils, preventing deployment in ministry on the basis of gender hampers the proclamation of the gospel and denies the biblical message of the priesthood of all believers. In the next article, I will study this issue more fully, along with Jesus' own example and antidote for victory over this spiritual axis of evil.

Defeating the Axis of Spiritual Evil— Part 2

In the previous article we discussed a spiritual axis of evil that many churches eagerly embrace despite the deadly consequences of allowing this unholy troika of racism, social distinction, and gender discrimination to dominate.

The evils of racism and social distinction. Whatever our excuse, racism and worship segregation plus overpopulation of judicatory boards and committees with those of enhanced socioeconomic status—while excluding those of whom God's Word declares, He chooses the poorer of this world to be rich in faith (see James 2:5)—remain as much evil today as they were when Paul admonished the church against these divisive sins (Galatians 3:27–29).

The evil of gender discrimination. Like these other sins, preventing deployment in ministry on the basis of gender hampers the proclamation of the gospel and denies a basic biblical doctrine of the priesthood of all believers.

The New Testament records how women have been utilized in many functions and offices since the very inception of the church. While the Seventh-day Adventist Church today does not ordain women to ministry, this decision appears to have been driven far more by ecclesiological policy of all denominational entities remaining unified in practics than by nonnegotiable theological imperatives.

Scripturally, the roles of prophet, elder, deacon, teacher, evangelist, pastor, bishop/administrator, and even apostle appear to be open for both genders as affirmed by church practice, apostolic declaration, and biblical affirmation. Prejudicial reasoning to the contrary, you will not find biblical support for excluding women from church leadership. On this, both Paul and Jesus are in complete accord. Jesus' own example—His personal ministry—thoroughly demonstrates this fact by one consequential episode (John 4) in which He destroyed all three man-made barriers.

"But He needed to go through Samaria" (verse 4, NKJV). Jesus actually went against the normal travel route from Jerusalem to Galilee in order to go through Samaria. Jews typically headed east, crossing over Jordan near Jericho in order to journey along the East Bank until well north of Samaria. Then, recrossing the river into Galilee, they avoided even the soil of the despised Samaritans. But Scripture declares the Lord had a purpose in mind. Jesus *needed* to go to Samaria.

The Gospel says, "Jesus therefore, being wearied from His journey, sat thus by the well. . . . A woman of Samaria came to draw water. Jesus said to her, 'Give Me a drink' " (verses 6, 7, NKJV).

Jesus eradicates racial boundaries. "Then the woman of Samaria said to Him, 'How is it that You, being a Jew, ask a drink from me, a Samaritan woman?' For Jews have no dealings with Samaritans" (verse 9, NKJV).

By instigating this one conversation, Jesus intentionally breached the taboo against Jews engaging Samaritans. He exemplified the theology of the apostle Paul, who declared that in Christ there is neither Jew nor Gentile (see Galatians 3:28).

Jesus eradicates social distinction boundaries. After discussing the availability of living water, the woman responded, " 'Sir, give me this water, that I may not thirst, nor come here to draw.' Jesus said to her, 'Go, call your husband, and come here.' The woman answered and said, 'I have no husband.' Jesus said to her, 'You have well said, "I have no husband," for you have had five husbands, and the one whom you now have is not your husband; in that you spoke truly.' The woman said to Him, 'Sir, I perceive that You are a prophet' " (John 4:15–19, NKJV).

For an individual of Jesus' perfect, unsullied nature to offer such a sinner both conversation and conversion demonstrates that no individual is beyond heaven's redemptive love and plan for discipleship. Despite her past and despite her present ongoing involvement with another's spouse, Jesus offered her the same acceptance He extends to every disciple. New life for a low life!

Jesus eradicates gender boundaries. The Lord called this new convert to proclaim the message of spiritual liberty for the captives. In utilizing this woman as the first-recorded public evangelist, Jesus clearly demonstrated that every believer possesses capacity and calling for ministry.

She was used by God just as Mary was used as the first preacher of the resurrected Lord. These women ministered, not just in prophetic roles, but in a proclamation. Clearly, God calls and uses women in ministry. The church should do no less.

And she was successful! The whole town was eager to hear her. What an evangelistic strategy for gathering a crowd! She advertised her message by saying, "He told me everything I've ever done!" "And many of the Samaritans of that city believed in Him because of the word of the woman who testified, 'He told me all that I ever did' " (verse 39, NKJV).

In my opinion, Jesus needed to go through Samaria in order to eradicate false concepts about who qualifies to minister. The Bible is clear. We are all one in Christ Jesus.

The Peril of Playing One Note

I increasingly suspect both individuals and entities that seem unable to move beyond the one note they have perfected. Rather than engaging a wide range of options theological, practical, or liturgical these "same songers" seem content, even committed, to repeating over and over their one noise until the brassy clanging becomes so familiar that volume is valued over substance.

> For in fact the body is not one member but many. . . . But now God has set the members, each one of them, in the body just as He pleased. . . . And the eye cannot say to the hand, "I have no need of you"; nor again the head to the feet, "I have no need of you." . . . There should be no schism in the body, but that the members should have the same care for one another. And if one member suffers, all the members suffer with it; or if one member is honored, all the members rejoice with it. Now you are the body of Christ, and members individually (1 Corinthians 12:14–27).

Recently, I have observed a few breakaway groups whose singular focus appears to be removing themselves further and further from the established body as they strive (and strife is typical of the process) to establish their independence. Unfortunately, those who embark on these ventures, typically slalom the same downhill slopes.

First, although they proclaim their intentions only to reform, they assert their own greater trustworthiness over established structures to manage tithes and offerings. In reality, their independence is from management and oversight by church leaders and policies rather than independence from the financial support by church members.

Then, in hopes of maintaining the initial surge of enthusiasm which seems to swarm like yellow jackets to warm lemonade, these groups begin to subtly distinguish their more pure theological views or enhanced applications of various doctrines or missions. The more convoluted their reasoning, the more successful they appear.

One such group, in the process of legally establishing itself as separate and independent from church structure has already abandoned the Great Commission of going to the world with the gospel and, instead, has begun to focus on going to various unions and conferences with initiatives to recruit the "already saved." Despite protestations to the contrary, these zealots, perhaps well-intentioned, are far more adventurers than Adventists. In addition, I also see the following dangerous deficiencies:

- No organizational or doctrinal unity among individual congregations.
- No organizational or doctrinal accountability. Heresy may freely develop in one congregation of such loosely linked fellowships with no power by others to call for repentance or reform.
- No support for pastors except by local congregations.
- No security for properties, buildings, institutions, etc.
- No safeguarding of initial theological educational processes for ministers.
- No plans to professionally develop or continually educate the clergy.
- No equitably balanced financial remuneration policies for pastor in large versus small assignments.
- No retirement system or healthcare benefits.
- No educational benefits for PKs and no parochial schools for any of the church's kids.
- No coordinated method for transferring, calling, ordaining, or disciplining workers. Everyone does what is right in their own eyes.
- No financial accountability to constituency sessions.
- No broad-based emphasis (i.e., laity training, family ministries, women's ministries, health ministries, publishing, etc.) in support of common values.
- Little stabilizing discipleship of new converts into responsible members focused on a worldview more than local growth. This neglect of steady spiritual discipline in favor of that which is the most new and exciting venture of the moment metastasizes uncontrolled, spreading here or there but seldom creating a vision beyond the borders of local province.

Why the impetus to self-directed independence? Individuals will often more easily pursue a course of action which they would have previously eschewed if a root of bitterness over perceived slights is nurtured and allowed to flourish. Life is always unfair this side of God's new creation and the urge to separate and operate independently of the authoritative body flourished even in Paradise with Lucifer's rebellion.

Differently Genuine

Typically, we fear something new and different for those very reasons. All humans embrace the familiar and routine and resist that which challenges our comfortable, long-established patterns. "After all," we reason, "we have always done it this way; it must be correct!"

When I rode the train nearly two hours north of Sydney to attend a recently planted church, I was not sure what to expect since I had heard many opinions ranging from "everything the wider church needs" to "precarious experimentation that cannot last."

My host, Pastor Wayne Krause, who also serves as director of the South Pacific Division's Center for Church Planting, had noted that I would not need a dress suit since most of the attendees would dress "casual." After three weeks of difficult travel itinerary, this expectation immediately made the entire venture much more appealing.

Although the church's location, just two blocks from the train station, was close enough to walk, the pastor met me, and we took a quick drive around the community of Wyong on Australia's central coast. Soon we circled back to a large facility that looked more like a warehouse than a cathedral. Signs identified the multiuse building as a district social hall, a Salvation Army Center, and Central Coast Community Church of Seventh-day Adventists (CCCC). The lack of abundant parking was less obvious because of close proximity to transit lines and several nearby parking lots.

Worship services are held first at CCCC with Bible Discovery (Sabbath School) following. Logically, this resonates with the needs of the many young families who attend "Big Church" and allows parents to worship together as a family before their kids become too restless to settle into a sermon/worship setting.

Following worship, the church clearly envisioned the needs of various groups. First, a delightful breakfast buffet greeted all attendees, as fellowship time extended into prayer groups, sharing, storytelling, discussions, and unrushed social and spiritual engagement. The church always provides a noon lunch as well.

Provisions for children included babysitting plus Kids' Church that was carefully themed to the adult study and worship. The youngsters enjoyed the lesson study in various ways, such as small groups, crafts, singing, mission story, and age-appropriate witnessing strategies. I was particularly impressed with the number of community kids who showed up at *their* church. This outreach strategy of high-quality children's programming works because kids bring their parents.

Adult study options included a general lesson study taught that day by the pastor who emphasized the fifteenth chapter of the Gospel of John, as well as the importance of orthodoxy coupled with outreach.

Various fellowship groups offer mutual and interactive support that spills over into other functions throughout the week, such as men's group at the local pub (a location selected for the purpose of interacting with the locals), prayer ministry, and various support groups.

Although the type of music played and sung was not my preference, it showed careful thought and thorough planning integral to worship preparation. Extraordinarily talented individuals, such as the original drummer from the band AC/DC—now a CCCC church member—led the congregational singing. A Bob Dylan song, sung just before the sermon, perfectly matched Pastor Krause's message that followed.

Two young adults, who had scheduled their baptisms, each shared powerful testimonies of their search for God and commitment to discipleship.

Attractively designed, free-standing banners, detailed CCCC's core values: inspiring worship, gift-based ministry, need-focused evangelism, Christlikeness, community, empowering leadership, process, excellence, passionate spirituality, holistic small groups, multiplication, encouragement, authenticity, love-acceptance-forgiveness, and relevance.

Wayne and Tracey Krause make mentoring a high priority for their ministry. Erika Gemmell, who served a year as assistant pastor, says, "I saw the church function in a totally different way than I'd ever seen before. People became alive as the body of Christ." She adds, "Pastor Krause mentored me and constantly challenged me to determine how I would apply what I experienced there in my future ministry. In the five years since, I have resolved that when a body of believers has a clear and focused mission, we become empowered to use our spiritual gifts for God's glory and to care for each other in His name. My experience clarified my understanding of God's call on my life."

The South Pacific Division should rejoice in this emphasis on innovative church planting. Although some have raised questions about the authenticity of CCCC's approach (primarily individuals who have never actually attended), I was pleased to discover a passion and clarity for both the message and mission of Adventist beliefs. I encourage others to discover for themselves the value of such needs-based ministry that struggles to involve the church community with local society in a way that abandons the *fortress mentality* of isolation from the world and embraces the *force mentality* that engages the world.

I summarize my CCCC experience in two words: *different* and *genuine!*

Slippery Slope

Prophecy indicates God's church of the last days will experience the same challenges as the early church. "Also from among yourselves men will rise up, speaking perverse things, to draw away the disciples after themselves" (Acts 20:30, NKJV).

The first steps down any slippery slope seldom appear dangerous. In fact, many begin a fatal spiral believing they are strengthening Christ's kingdom and following God's will. However, most independent groups follow virtually the same tragic path.

Good intentions. Even worthy plans need the balance of the entire body. Scripture warns against one body part attempting to be all or do all. Nothing is quite so dangerous as someone with only one good idea. Despite their best attempts to reform the church, such narrow focus rejects a broader picture or varying viewpoints and ends up harming the very body they intended to enhance. "These one-idea men can see nothing except to press the one thing that presents itself to their mind."[1]

Reject counsel. Refusing the counsel of leadership demonstrates disregard for the God of heaven who places individuals in positions of responsibility. Although God does not require uniformity of opinion or methodology, an independent spirit which rejects good advice reflects more the sociological attitudes of our culture than spirituality, or even creativity. "These devoted souls consider it a virtue to boast of their freedom to think and act independently. They will not take any man's say-so. They are amenable to no man. I was shown that it is Satan's special work to lead men to feel that it is God's order for them to strike out for themselves and choose their own course independent of their brethren."[2]

Harbor resentments. Corrective guidance, perceived insults, slights—whether real or imagined—too easily form a root of bitterness which poisons the once-tender mind until fruitful ministry is devoured. "Pursue peace with all people, and holiness, without which no one will see the Lord: looking carefully lest anyone fall short of the grace of God; lest any root of bitterness springing up cause trouble,

---

1. Ellen G. White, *Evangelism* (Hagerstown, Md.: Review and Herald®, 1946), 216.

2. White, *Testimonies to Ministers and Gospel Workers* (Nampa, Idaho: Pacific Press®, 1923), 29.

and by this many become defiled" (Hebrews 12:14, 15, NKJV).

More responsible management. Unchecked, such resentments soon metastasize into expressed opinions that the organized church cannot be trusted to expend the finances through voted, budgeted, and audited processes. Advocacy of independent agendas and personal priorities soon ripens into receiving offerings, soliciting tithe, and attacking others. Fervent solicitations disguise irresponsibility, unvoted priorities, and undocumented utilization.

Narrowed focus. Independents, concentrating on recruiting individuals or resources from the established church, inevitably neglect the wider task of winning the lost. Self-focused interests become so consuming that the very evangelistic mission which may have originally propelled their agenda is neglected.

Subtle distinctions. Independents quickly realize the brevity of their window of opportunity to recruit the attention and money of loyal members. Even while professing adherence to the doctrines and mission of the church, they urge subtle distinctions designed to demonstrate their holier, historical position. Typically, these are minor points blown out of proportion into major issues. "We sought most earnestly that the Scriptures should not be wrested to suit any man's opinions. We tried to make our differences as slight as possible by not dwelling on points that were of minor importance, upon which there were varying opinions." . . . "Men will make a world of an atom and an atom of a world."[3]

Masked disloyalty. Claims of loyalty to God's prophetic gift, presents an appearance of piety, devotion, and education. Lengthy quotations are selected to substantiate assertions of error. "It will be found that those who bear false messages will not have a high sense of honor and integrity. They will deceive the people, and mix up with their error the Testimonies of Sister White, and use her name to give influence to their work. They make such selections from the Testimonies as they think they can twist to support their positions, and place them in a setting of falsehood, so that their error may have weight and be accepted by the people."[4]

Belief abandonment. Downsliding is as spiritually dangerous as backsliding. Remember, slipping and sliding is never skiing or sledding. If it seems easier to continue careening down the slope than to accept heaven's help to change, pray for the Holy Spirit to reveal your spirit of godless independence. If tempted to follow such sophistries, remember: "He [God] is leading, not stray offshoots, not one here and one there, but a people."[5]

---

3. Ibid., 25, 165.
4. Ibid., 42.
5. Ibid., 61.